Southern Mountain Folksongs

Southern Mountain Folksongs

*Traditional Songs
from the Appalachians
and the Ozarks*

W.K. McNeil

This volume is a part of
The American Folklore Series
W.K. McNeil, General Editor

August House Publishers, Inc.
LITTLE ROCK

Printed in the United States of America

10 9 8 7 6 5 4 3 2 1

LIBRARY OF CONGRESS CATALOGING-IN-PUBLICATION DATA
Southern mountain folksongs : traditional songs from the Appalachians
and the Ozarks / [compiled by] W.K. McNeil. — 1st ed.
p.   cm. — (The American folklore series)
Melodies; includes words printed as text.
Introd. and notes on each song by McNeil.
Includes bibliographical references.
ISBN 0–87483–284–5 (HB) : $24.95
ISBN 0–87483–285–3 (PB) : $14.95
1. Folk music—Appalachian Region.
2. Folk music—Ozark Mountains Region.
3. Folk songs, English—Appalachian Region.
4. Folk songs, English—Ozark Mountains Region.
I. McNeil, W.K.   II. Series
M1629.S72 1992   92-36617

First Edition, 1993

Executive editor: Liz Parkhurst
Series editor: W.K. McNeil
Design director: Ted Parkhurst
Cover design: Byron Taylor
Typography: Lettergraphics / Little Rock

This book is printed on archival-quality paper which meets the
guidelines for performance and durability of the Committee on
Production Guidelines for Book Longevity of the
Council on Library Resources.

AUGUST HOUSE, INC.   PUBLISHERS   LITTLE ROCK

To the memory of Rose P. Rigdon
who always loved a good song
whether it told a story or not

Guide to Reading Musical Notation

(1) All folksongs are transcribed exactly as performed at the time of collection, even though there may be some irregularities in time, rhythm, and notation.

(2) Time signatures enclosed in parentheses indicate that there will be variations from the stated time within the folksong.

(3) A short bar under a note indicates that that note is to be played or sung with special emphasis.

Contents

Acknowledgments

ONE OF THE NICEST THINGS about completing a manuscript is that the author gets to acknowledge the help of all those who aided him. Such contributions are essential because no matter how resourceful or knowledgeable a writer or editor may be, at some point it is necessary to rely on the generosity, patience, and knowledge of others. For the present volume several individuals deserve special mention for their selflessness and willingness to come to my aid, even though doing so meant that some of them had to put their own projects temporarily on hold. For their valuable contributions I gratefully acknowledge Dan Brackin, Irene Jones Carlisle, Dianne Dugaw, Theodore Garrison, Loyal Jones, Charles K. Wolfe, and Tom Baskett, Jr., for his editorial advice. They are, of course, not responsible for any errors that may be contained here.

Introduction

IN AT LEAST TWO WAYS this book is different from most others dealing with traditional songs. With a few exceptions, other volumes treating this topic are devoted exclusively or largely to ballads—songs that tell a chronological story. An overwhelming majority of these books deal with the traditional songs found within a single state, a region, or the entire nation. *Southern Mountain Folksongs* departs from these works by focusing solely on non-narrative traditional songs found in two regions of the United States, the Ozarks and southern Appalachia.[1] These two areas have strong connections, historically and in the minds of many people. Indeed, both public and scholars often think of the Ozarks as Appalachia West.[2] For reasons which will be explained later, that is an erroneous view, no matter how convincing it is to some. But it does suggest there is justification for lumping the two regions together in an examination of cultural traditions, be they folksong or some other aspect of folklore.

This collection of folksongs was recorded primarily since 1950 in the Ozarks and Appalachia. Most are widely popular and are known in both regions, but a few have been reported only from one of the two mountain sections. For many reasons it is unwise to say that songs are not known in places where they have not been reported. To my knowledge, no collector has ever claimed to record every single item known in a region, much less accomplished such a goal. The very nature of folksongs makes determining whether or not such a feat was achieved virtually impossible, even if some collector might be inclined to make the claim. Folksongs are very fluid, and individual elements get attached to a variety of songs; thus, some lines may be widely known even if the entire song's popularity is limited to a relatively small area. So frequently do lyrics move from one song to another that knowing which specific song they belong to often is difficult. Obviously, this feature also complicates making the decision whether or not a song is known in a region.

Several of the songs in this book come from my own fieldwork, but most are from other collections and archives. Some of them may have originated in the Ozarks and Appalachia, but most did not. Instead, they had their origins in various places ranging from the Old World to the American commercial popular music industry. While some are several centuries old, most do not predate 1800. These certainly aren't the only folksongs known in Appalachia or the Ozarks, but the six basic types presented here do represent the most popular themes found in the folksong repertoires of the two regions. Each song in the book has been maintained by oral tradition and is thus an example of a folksong.

Many readers may find several of the terms used in this volume unfamiliar, confusing, or unclear. First is the word *folklore,* which in popular usage is generally reserved for anything quaint or odd. That is not the exact meaning of the word, however, and not the one used in this book. Here, folklore refers to material that is passed on orally, informally, and becomes traditional; undergoes change over space and time, creating variants and versions; is anonymous in the sense that most bearers of folklore are not concerned with who the original creator was, or even that there *was* an original creator; and finally, usually is formulaic.[3]

For present purposes, it is essential to discuss exactly what territory is covered by the Ozarks and Appalachia. Most readers undoubtedly have a general idea where the two regions lie but may be uncertain about the precise boundaries. They can hardly be faulted for that since there is disagreement even among scholars who specialize in studying Appalachia and the Ozarks. In the case of both mountain regions, there is a relatively small, exclusive drawing of the boundary lines and a larger, more inclusive setting of the borders, both of which have their ardent adherents. Thus, depending on who one listens to, Appalachia consists of as few as 190 counties in seven states or an many as 230 counties in nine states. I use the larger region in this book—as defined here, Appalachia includes portions of Maryland, Virginia, Kentucky, North Carolina, South Carolina, Tennessee, Georgia, and Alabama, and all of West Virginia. The most exclusive definition of the geographical extent of the Ozarks is that the region covers most of northern Arkansas and southern Missouri; the most inclusive holds that it takes in those two areas plus portions of eastern Oklahoma, southeastern Kansas, and southern Illinois. In the present volume, I use the broader boundaries.[4]

Appalachia was named much earlier than the Ozarks, but, interestingly, European-Americans settled the Ozarks earlier. For more than four centuries people have known of the Appalachians. In 1540, Spanish explorer Hernando de Soto, who became lost in the southern Blue Ridge, reportedly named the mountains for the Apalachee Indians who hindered his approach to the area. Twenty-nine years later, in 1569, cartographer Gerardus Mercator fairly accurately located a mountain area that he called "Apalechen" in his "New and Improved Description of the Lands of the World." A century later, English traders were regularly traveling through the mountains, and by 1750 the various Appalachian ridges were being accurately situated on maps. For many years the mountains were considered a barrier to westward settlement, but around the middle of the eighteenth century, some whites living in Pennsylvania moved into the Appalachians through a break in the Blue Ridge. These first settlers were followed by many others, but it was still almost a century before there were a million non-Indian settlers in Appalachia.[5]

It is uncertain both where the name *Ozark* comes from or when the word was coined, though there have been a number of theories offered about the former. Most of these have to do with an Anglicization of a French phrase.[6] It is generally agreed that *Ozark*, which does not otherwise occur in the English language, first became widely used in reference to the mountain region in the 1820s. The first European-American settlers, however, came in the early eighteenth century when Frenchmen moved into the northern Ozarks in Missouri. Salt springs and lead ore in the area attracted permanent settlements by 1704. But, while they were not the first whites in the region, immigrants from the southern uplands have played a main role in shaping the traditional heritage of the Ozarks. Motivated in part by land grants to descendants of Revolutionary

War and War of 1812 soldiers, people from eastern Tennessee, southeastern Kentucky, southwestern Virginia, and other parts of Appalachia began moving into the Ozarks in large numbers during the decades just before the Civil War. So influential has this cultural group been in shaping Ozark history and folklore that it is popularly believed they are the only significant cultural group in Ozark history. Those who accept this idea regard the Ozarks as a cultural carbon copy of Appalachia, a notion that is clearly wrong. Obviously, much of Ozark culture is derived from Appalachia, but many other groups also have contributed to the whole.

Certainly Appalachia and the Ozarks share many cultural features, of which a few merit discussion here. One of the most important is that neither region is homogeneous, despite claims to the contrary made by many past scholars. There is no such thing as Appalachian or Ozark culture in the sense of traits uniformly held throughout either region; actually, it is more accurate to think of Appalachian and Ozark cultures. A second distinctive characteristic of Appalachia and the Ozarks is that both sections are rural, although the Ozarks is more sparsely populated than Appalachia. The two regions, of course, have their urban places, such as Knoxville in eastern Tennessee and Asheville in western North Carolina and the Fayetteville-Springdale area in Arkansas, but the general nature of daily life in both mountain areas is rural. A third distinctive feature shared by Ozark and Appalachian residents is a well-defined sense of place. While experts may not agree on exact boundaries of the two regions, the people who live there know whether or not they are Ozarkers or Appalachian mountaineers. In many communities in the two regions, one is not regarded as a "true" insider unless he or she is born in the region. Sometimes—but not usually—this cultural attitude is carried to extremes and there is real hostility towards outsiders.

Another cultural trait characteristic of Appalachia and the Ozarks that deserves mention is the relative stability of the social systems. One cultural geographer has pictured the Ozarks in this way—and could just as well have been writing about Appalachia:

> Things are relatively uncomplicated. There are strong and stable
> kinship relations that extend back generations. Social activities

focus on schools and churches, and these institutions are depend-
able and predictable. Ozarkers know who their friends are and
who their enemies are and what to do about it. There are few ego
problems or questions about belonging.[7]

A final term that must be defined is *folksong,* a word that is
especially important for the present book. It is used in two ways by
folklorists, first as a generic word applied to all songs passed on by
folksingers, and second to distinguish between lyric and narrative
songs. *Ballad* is the term applied to traditional songs that tell a story,
while *folksong* is reserved for those numbers that do not contain a
narrative. The question is how much narrative does a song need to
be called a ballad rather than a folksong? A song such as "Swing and
Turn Jubilee," made up entirely of "floating verses" (that is, verses
found in numerous songs and seemingly fitting all equally well),
probably would not be mistaken for a ballad even by novice
folksong specialists. As the lyrics make evident, it simply doesn't tell
a connected narrative: it does suggest some story but never goes
beyond the hint.

> *It's all out on the old railroad,*
> *It's all out on the sea.*
> *It's all out on the old railroad,*
> *As far as I can see.*
> *Swing and turn jubilee,*
> *Live and learn jubilee.*
>
> *Wished I had a big white horse,*
> *Corn to feed him on.*
> *Pretty little girl to stay at home*
> *And feed him when I'm gone.*
> *Swing and turn jubilee,*
> *Live and learn jubilee.*
>
> *If I had no horse to ride,*
> *I'd be down a crawlin'*
> *Up and down this rocky road*
> *Lookin' for my darlin'.*
> *Swing and turn jubilee,*
> *Live and learn jubilee.*

Hardest work I ever done
Was working on the farm.
Easiest work I ever done
Was swing my true love's arm.
Swing and turn jubliee,
Live and learn jubilee.

Some will come on Saturday night;
Some will come on Sunday.
If you give them half a chance,
They'll be back on Monday.
Swing and turn jubilee,
Live and learn jubilee.

Wished I had a needle and thread
As fine as I could sew.
I'd sew the girls to my coat tails
And 'round the room I'd go.
Swing and turn jubilee,
Live and learn jubilee.[8]

Likewise, it seems doubtful that any specialist would classify the song "Drunkard's Hell" as anything other than a ballad.

One awful dark and stormy night,
I heard, I saw an awful sight,
The lightnin' flashed, the thunder rolled
Around my aching, weary soul.

I saw a crowd far down below,
Where all the dying drunkards go.
This is my home, no tongue can tell
The horrible sight of a drunkard's hell.

The next saloon I staggered past,
I thought I'd take a sociable glass.
Every time I'd think it well
I'd think about that drunkard's hell.

I dashed it down and left that place.
I thought I'd seek redeeming grace.
But every time I'd think it well
I'd think about that drunkard's hell.

I started home to change my life,
To see my own elected wife.
I found her weeping by our bed
Because our little babe was dead.

I said, "Dear wife don't mourn and weep."
"Our little babe is just asleep.
Its little soul has passed away
To dwell with Christ through an endless day."

I taken her by her small white hand,
She was so weak she could not stand.
She then knelt down to say a prayer
That God might come and save us there.

Oh, girls, turn down the drinking man
While yet you may, while yet you can.
There's many a girl who's sad today
Because in poverty she lived and stayed.[9]

There are, however, many other songs that are not so obviously in one camp or the other. For example, consider the following three songs, "Sourwood Mountain," "Bring Back My Blue-Eyed Boy," and "Waggoner's Lad."

I've got a girl in the Sourwood mountains;
She's gone cripple an' blin'.
She's broke the heart of many a pore feller
But she ain't broken this 'n o' mine.

I've got a girl in the bend o' the river,
Tink-tank-toodle all the day.
A hop and a jump and I'll be with her,
Tink-tank-toodle all the day.

I've got a love in the Buffalo holler,
Tink-tank-toodle all the day.
She wouldn't come an' it's I won't call her,
Tink-tank-toodle all the day.

Now my love went a-floatin' down the river,
Tink-tank-toodle all the day.
If I had my boat I'd 'a' went with her,
Tink-tank-toodle all the day.

An old grey goose went a-swimmin' down the river,
Tink-tank-toodle all the day.
If I was a gander I'd a went with her,
Tink-tank-toodle all the day.

Big dog bark, little dog bite you,
Tink-tank-toodle all the day.
Big girl court and little girl slight you,
Tink-tank-toodle all the day.

I got a girl in the head of the holler,
Tink-tank-toodle all the day.
She won't come and I won't foller,
Tink-tank-toodle all the day.

She sits up with old Si Hall,
Tink-tank-toodle all the day.
Me and Jeff can't go there at all,
Tink-tank-toodle all the day.

Some of these days before very long
Tink-tank-toodle all the day.
I'll get that girl and a-home I'll run
Tink-tank-toodle all the day. [10]

* * * *

Remember well and bear in mind,
That a good true friend is hard to find.
And when you find that one is true,
Change not the old one for the new.

Go bring me back my blue-eyed boy.
Go bring my darling back to me.
Go bring me back my blue-eyed boy
And happy will I ever be.

Oh, I loved him once and I love him still,
I love him now and I always will.
His loving thoughts, his winning ways,
Are in my heart and there it stays.

Oh, who on earth can be my friend?
And who can hold my little white hand?
And who can kiss my ruby lips
When I am in a distant land?

Oh, mama she can be my friend,
And poppa can hold my little white hand.
And you may kiss my ruby lips
When I am in a distant land.

Your love is like a little bird
That flies from tree and unto tree,
For the loss of one and the gain of two,
And that is why I married you.[11]

* * * *

I am a poor girl, my fortune is sad
I've always been courted by a waggoner's lad.
He courted me gaily, by night and by day
And now he is loaded and going away.

Your horses are hungry, go feed them some hay.
Come sit down here by me as long as you stay.
My horses ain't hungry, they won't eat your hay.
So fare you well, darling, I'll be on my way.

Your wagon needs greasing your whip needs to mend.
Come sit down here by me as long as you can.
My wagon is greasy, my whip's in my hand,
So fare you well darling, I'll no longer stand.[12]

Most folksong specialists probably would not classify either of the first two numbers as ballads, but the last one is often so categorized. Yet even the most superficial observer would likely say that the first two songs contain at least as much, if not more, of a story than the last one. That being the case, why is the latter one called a ballad while the first two songs aren't? The answer is that most folksong specialists have followed the lead of the eighteenth-century poet William Shenstone, who referred to ballads as those songs in which action predominates over sentiment.[13] In actual practice, though, classification often proves to be arbitrary. Thus, Celestin P. Cambiaire categorizes a version of "Waggoner's Lad" as a ballad, while the editors of *The Frank C. Brown Collection of North Carolina Folklore* list it as a folksong.[14]

Because ballads provide narratives, they are relatively easy to identify and so have received considerable study. A number of classification systems have been devised for various types of ballads, the monumental one being Francis James Child's ten-volume *The English and Scottish Popular Ballads* (1882-1898). Child felt that in this, his magnum opus, he achieved his major goal of providing "every valuable copy of every known ballad."[15] His assessment was, of course, overly optimistic; but, given his specific definitions, few other examples of ballads have been discovered in the more than ninety years since his tenth, and last, volume appeared. This lack of success, however, is partly because for most of this time no one was looking for new ballads of the type catalogued by Child. For more than fifty years after Child's final volume appeared, folksong collectors throughout the country prized the Child ballads above all other ballads and folksongs and sought out variants and versions of them, in many instances ignoring everything else. As recently as 1956, an Appalachian folklore collector stated that "the genuine *ballad* is only one type of folksong. Your ballad is not a true *folk* ballad unless it is closely kin to one of the 305—no more, no less!—in Professor Child's great collection."[16]

Prior to the publication of Child's multi-volume work, little collecting of traditional songs, whether ballads or folksongs, was conducted in America. In fact, much of the subsequent collecting was stimulated by the Child canon. There are, of course, many reasons why the ten-volume set prompted so much fieldwork. Some people may have been challenged by Child's suggestion that ballad singing was, for all practical purposes, a dead issue. Specifically, Child said that although he tried to obtain texts from field collecting in Scotland, Canada, and the United States, the "gathering from tradition has been, as ought perhaps to have been foreseen at this late day, meager, and generally of indifferent quality."[17] Such a statement almost begs to be challenged, and subsequent field collections have proven that Child was premature in announcing the demise of traditional ballad singing.

Many collectors also undoubtedly agreed with Child that the 305 ballads he compiled were the best of the traditional balladry from the British Isles. But perhaps the main reason *The English and Scottish Popular Ballads* stimulated so much collecting is that it was a mammoth, accessible reference work that provided a convenient classification system. Scholars in folklore, as in other disciplines, tend to concern themselves primarily with matters their predecessors were concerned with. Of course, in the quest for versions and variants of Child ballads, some other traditional songs were gathered from folksingers. Many of the other narrative songs were eventually classified in two works by the University of Pennsylvania scholar G. Malcolm Laws. His *Native American Balladry* (1950) and *American Balladry From British Broadsides* (1957) were offered as merely bibliographic guides and syllabi. Thus, Laws avoided Child's extreme claim of completeness; but even so, the two books have been elevated to the status of canons by users who have treated their general groupings as though they were systematic classifications. Yet unlike Child's ten volumes, the two Laws books have not provided the immediate impetus for much subsequent field-collecting.

To date, no work has even been attempted that performs a similar service for folksongs that Child's ten-volume work and the two books by Laws provide for ballads. Indeed, very few books have appeared that are devoted exclusively to non-narrative songs, and those that have are collections rather than classification systems or bibliographic guides. The earliest, and largest, such American work is the third volume of *The Frank C. Brown Collection of North*

Carolina Folklore (1952), and its editors, Henry M. Belden and Arthur Palmer Hudson, admit that their categorizing of the 658 numbers in the collection as folksongs rather than ballads often is arbitrary:

> The composite and desultory character of a great deal of traditional folk song makes a strictly logical classification of the items impossible. But the items must be placed in *some* order. If a given piece is found among the ballads when it seems to be rather merely a song, or vice versa—if the placing of items seems sometimes merely arbitrary—we must plead necessity.[18]

While there has been no Child-like classification system proposed for folksongs in general, there have been a few studies of individual folksongs. Unfortunately, most of these remain unpublished, but one that is available is Tristram P. Coffin's investigation of "Green Grows the Laurel."[19] Taking a very popular folksong, Coffin proposes a method for making sense of the "endlessly wandering groups of stanzas, interchange of cliché, and lack of plotted action" in lyric songs. He suggests the most fruitful avenue is to determine the identifying element in the song and then do historic-geographic study of identifiable lyrics, much as was once done with folktales.[20] Through this means, one can establish the main types and patterns of diffusion. "Green Grows the Laurel" was chosen primarily because it is a "typical folk lyric," and therein lies one of the problems. It is just a little too ideal; that is, the song's core is much easier to determine than those of many folksongs. Furthermore, Coffin deals only with the chorus, but it is more problematic analyzing the several verses that are attached to this song.

Far more extensive than Coffin's article is the yet-unpublished study by Judith McCulloh of "In the Pines."[21] In this 650-page work, McCulloh analyzes both the tunes and the lyrics for 160 versions of an American lyric song in an attempt to answer the question, When can a song be confidently identified as "In the Pines"? She concludes that in order to qualify, a number must have four identifying elements, one musical and three textual. The musical element is the tune most often associated with "In the Pines," and the three textual elements are the phrases "in the pines, in the pines, where the sun never shines," "the longest train I ever saw," and a group of verses briefly describing an accident in which someone is beheaded. McCulloh follows Coffin's lead in determining the identifying elements of the song but goes further than just examining a single stanza to analyze verses from each of the numerous texts of "In the Pines" that she has compiled, and she also gives greater attention to the melodies. Her far-ranging analysis gives McCulloh's conclusions great authority. Her work and Coffin's give some indication of the value of close examinations of folksongs and provide important starting points for future research in this area.

Some scholars incline to the view that there are no folksongs, only ballads. They reason that all songs in oral tradition originally told a story, but that over time some have lost their narrative and consist only of bits and pieces of the original song. This concept, however, is not accepted by most contemporary authorities. Some scholars do classify as ballads songs that focus on an event but do not tell a complete story. Such songs assume the audience has prior knowledge of the story so that only allusions—possibly with some moral commentary—are made to the details. The following version of a Scottish lament, which focuses on the sense of loss resulting from the Earl of Moray's death rather than the events by which the killing took place, provides one example:

> *Ye Highlands and ye Lowlands, it's where have ye been?*
> *Oh, they've slain the Earl of Mo-ray and laid him on the ground.*
>
> *Oh, he was a handsome feller, and wore a leather glove.*
> *Oh, the bonny Earl of Mo-ray he was the Queen's love.*
>
> *He was a noble rider, a-ridin' through the town,*
> *And all the pretty ladies they watched him up and down.*
>
> *He was a gallant player, a-playin' at the ball;*
> *Oh, the bonny Earl of Mo-ray was the flower of them all.*
>
> *He was a handsome feller and wore a golden ring.*
> *Oh, the bonny Earl of Mo-ray he ort to a been king.*[22]

The following version of "Tom Dula," dealing with a murderer hanged in 1868 at Statesville, North Carolina, is told from the viewpoint of a man about to die. Indeed, the singer said Dula wrote the song while in prison awaiting his execution. The song reflects on his deeds rather than describing them, presumably because the events would be well known to any local audience.

> *I pick my banjo now,*
> *I pick it on my knee.*
> *This time tomorrow night*
> *It'll be no more use to me.*
>
> *The banjo's been my friend*
> *In days both dark and ill.*
> *A-layin' here in jail*
> *It's helped me time to kill.*
>
> *Poor Laura loved its tunes*
> *When sitting 'neath a tree;*
> *I'd play and sing to her,*
> *My head upon her knee.*
>
> *Poor Laura loved me well,*
> *She was both fond and true;*
> *How deep her love for me*
> *I never really knew.*
>
> *Her black curl on my heart,*
> *I'll meet my fatal doom,*
> *As swift as she met hers*
> *That dreadful evening's gloom.*
>
> *I've lived my life of sin,*
> *I've had a bit of fun.*
> *Come, Ann, kiss me goodby,*
> *My race is nearly run.*[23]

Somewhere between "goodnight" ballads such as "Tom Dula" and the ballad proper are songs that some folklorists call "blues ballads." Although D.K. Wilgus is generally credited with coining this term, it was used sometime before 1925 by W.C. Handy, the self-proclaimed "Father of the Blues." Handy referred to his copyrighted song "Loveless Love" as a "blues ballad."[24] According to Wilgus, the "blues ballad" depends on a point of narrative reference, such as an actual event taking place in a community, that is known to the local audience for which the song is intended. Thus freed from the necessity of recounting the story, the ballad performer "concentrates on conventionalized dramatic scenes, oblique delineation of character through action and speech, and lyrical comment by characters or the narrator."[25] To illustrate his point, Wilgus uses the following song dealing with the 1895 slaying of Archibald Dixon Brown, son of Kentucky governor John Young Brown, by Fulton Gordon, his paramour's husband:

> *When Archie went to Louisville,*
> *When Archie went to Louisville,*
> *When Archie went to Louisville,*
> *Not thinking that he would be killed.*
>
> *When Gordon made his first shot,*
> *When Gordon made his first shot,*
> *When Gordon made his first shot,*
> *O'er behind the bed Arch did drop.*
>
> *Arch says, "Gordon, I didn't mean no harm."*
> *Arch says, "Gordon, I didn't mean no harm."*
> *Arch says, "Gordon, I didn't mean no harm."*
> *When Gordon shot Arch in the right arm.*
>
> *Hush now Guv'nor, don't you cry.*
> *Hush now Guv'nor, don't you cry.*
> *Hush now Guv'nor, don't you cry.*
> *You know your son Arch has to die.*
>
> *Now you see what a sporting life has done,*
> *Now you see what a sporting life has done,*
> *Now you see what a sporting life has done,*
> *It has killed Guv'nor Brown's only son.*[26]

Obviously, this type of ballad is closer in style to the folksong than to the ballad proper.

Folksongs, like ballads, have several distinctive characteristics, the most frequently noted being their amorphous form. Ballads hold together because they tell a chronological story that has a specific beginning, climax, and ending. Folksongs, by contrast, frequently seem unorganized. Indeed, one scholar comments that "folk lyric often appears beyond definition and even description."[27] But, as already noted, many ballads are just as amorphous and often lack a real story. The ballad Child called "The Lass of Roch Royal" tells a story about Isabel of Rochroyal, who goes with her newborn child to find her lover, Gregory. Arriving at Gregory's door, she is greeted by his mother, who refuses to believe Isabel is her son's sweetheart. She tells Isabel that Gregory has another love and closes the door. When Gregory finds out what his mother has done, he curses her and sets off to find Isabel. He arrives just in time to find his love's ship wrecked and both Isabel and their child drowned. After considerable mourning, Gregory dies of a broken heart. This very romantic tale is almost never encountered in American tradition; instead, most reported versions consist of lines like the following:

> *Oh who will shoe my foot, my love?*
> *An' who will glove my hand?*
> *An' who will kiss my ruby lips?*
> *While you're in that far-off land?*
>
> *Your father will shoe your little feet,*
> *Your mother will glove your hand,*
> *An' I will kiss your ruby lips*
> *When I return from that far-off land.*
>
> *If I prove false to you, my love,*
> *The rocks will melt in the sun,*
> *The fire its breeze shall blow no more,*
> *An' the ragin' sea shall burn.*[28]

Obviously, no chronological narrative is contained in this text and there is no beginning, climax, or end, because all verses are of equal importance. All that is given is a set of "floating verses" shared by at least thirty other songs. Nothing of the ancient tale found in Child's several texts appears in most American texts, yet lines such as these are invariably cited as versions of Child 76. The reason is that people assume the "who will shoe my foot" stanzas originated with the Child ballad, making it a ballad whether there is a narrative or not.

It actually is inaccurate to think of folksongs as lacking shape or meaning, for they do have a coherence, if not one based on dramatic focus. Instead, the lyrics of folksongs are organized around a central idea or ideas—the stanzas not chosen randomly, even though to many observers that may seem to be the case. In some instances, lyrics may be given in any order as long as they contribute to the overall idea of the folksong. Thus, in "The Arkansas Run," a song included in this book, the several verses support the general notion that girls from Missouri should be careful when courted by Arkansas boys, mainly because of the latter's poverty. Some folksongs, however, almost always have stanzas arranged in a specific order so as to present certain definite ideas. Thus, most versions of "Old Smokey" begin like the following text with the idea of slow courtship, then proceed to the thieflike qualities of a false-hearted lover, then state why such a love is worse than a thief:

> *On the top of Old Smokey,*
> *All covered in snow,*
> *I lost my true lover*
> *By courting too slow.*
>
> *Courting was pleasure,*
> *But parting was grief.*
> *A false-hearted lover*
> *Is worse than a thief.*
>
> *A thief he will rob you*
> *And take what you save,*
> *But a false-hearted lover*
> *Place you in the grave.*

The grave will decay you
And turn you to dust.
Not a boy in ten thousand
That a poor girl can trust.

They will tell you they love you
To give your heart ease,
And when your back's turned upon them
They'll court whom they please.

It's raining, it's hailing,
The moon gives no light.
Your horses can't travel
This dark stormy night.

So put up your horses
And feed them some hay.
Come and sit here beside me
As long as you stay.

'My horses ain't hungry,
They won't eat your hay.
I'll drive on, my true love,
And feed on my way.'

As sure as the dew drops
Fall on the green corn
My lover was with me;
But now he is gone.

So back to Old Smokey,
Old Smokey so high,
Where the wild birds and turtle doves
Can hear my sad cry.[29]

Whereas ballads focus on events, folksongs are organized around a situation or mood. Thus, the following text of "Rattler Treed a 'Possum" suggests a hunting scene:

Rattler treed a 'possum,
Rattler treed a 'possum,
Rattler treed a 'possum,
Up a 'simmon tree.

Raccoon and a 'possum,
Raccoon and a 'possum,
Raccoon and a 'possum,
In a hollow log.

Raccoon said to the 'possum,
Raccoon said to the 'possum,
Raccoon said to the 'possum,
"Let's hear that old hound dog."

Rattler treed a 'possum,
Rattler treed a 'possum,
Rattler treed a 'possum,
In a hollow log.[30]

"Rattlesnake Bill," on the other hand, contains the macho boasting of a protagonist who obviously considers himself a tough "ladies man":

My name is Rattlesnake Bill,
I was raised in a rattlesnake den.
My daily occupation all of my life
Was taking women from big old men.
And I wonder how long
They're gonna let me live.

CHORUS:
When I make this world do as I say,
I wonder if they'll let me by myself
When I tear this world to pieces.

I was walking down the road one day
And I thought I was by myself.
I grabbed a big lion by the tail
And there was nothing but sausage left.
And I wonder how long they're gonna let me live.

I was walking down the road one day
And I didn't mean any harm.
George jumped through the barbed wire fence
And John tore down the barn.
Just a-getting away from Rattlesnake Bill.

The further up on Rattlesnake Creek
The worser grow the men.
I live up in the very last house,
So, gee, what a man I am.
And I wonder how long they're gonna let me live.[31]

Several characteristics of folksongs are shared with ballads, including some types of repetition. The two most commonly found in Ozark and Appalachian folksongs are plain repetition, with words, phrases, or stanzas simply repeated, and the listing of family members. The song "The Arkansas Run," given elsewhere in this volume, is an example of the former; while "Go Wash in That Beautiful Pool," also in this book, is an example of the latter. Religious songs most commonly use this type of naming repetition, but it is found in others as well.

Two other characteristics of Ozark and Appalachian folksongs merit mention here. One is that the songs often are advanced by means of a monologue addressed to an unnamed party. Frequently, the person for whom it is intended obviously is a lover or all lovers, but there are other potential intended audiences. In the case of some songs, particularly those that are humorous, it is difficult to ascertain exactly what specific audience a song's lyrics are meant for. The second feature worth noting is that several folksongs have formulaic beginning stanzas and tend to rely on floating verses to a much greater extent than is the case with ballads. This is hardly surprising, for such techniques are commonly used as mnemonic (memory) devices by traditional singers, who find them especially important in non-narrative songs. Lacking a chronological narrative to guide them in the selection of lyrics, singers resort to formulaic opening lines and floating verses as convenient means of remembering songs. Two popular formulaic opening lines are "come all ye" and "remember well and bear in mind," but many others are commonly heard as well in Appalachia and the Ozarks. On the other hand, there are numerous folksongs traditional to the two regions that lack such standardized beginnings.

Although it is hard to be absolutely certain about the age of folksongs, it seems that the vast majority of those known in Appalachia and the Ozarks are of relatively recent vintage, going back no more than a couple of hundred years. Whether this holds for folksongs from other sections of the United States is unknown, but it well may. There is no evidence that suggests songs or individual lyrics predating 1790 are more or less popular than those developed after that time, although admittedly no one has really attempted any systematic study of degrees of popularity of either ballads or folksongs in Appalachia or the Ozarks. This relatively recent age of folksongs seems in direct contrast to the age of folk ballads in the two regions—especially when one considers that some narrative songs can be traced back four centuries. Even so, the bulk of the folk ballads from the Ozarks and Appalachia are of more recent date. For every "Barbara Allen" dating back to the seventeenth century, there are three ballads like "Daisy Deane," "The Girl That Wore a Waterfall," and "The Old Elm Tree" that are from the nineteenth century and several, such as "The Titanic," that are of even more recent origin.

Because many people think of the Ozarks and Appalachia as culturally identical, there may be a tendency to assume that the folksong repertoire of the two regions is identical. I believe that there are great similarities between what is sung traditionally in Appalachia and in the Ozarks, but that it is a mistake to assume the repertoires are exactly the same. Many songs are common to one area and not known in the other. "Banjo Pickin' Girl," for example, seems to be indigenous to Appalachia and is not known traditionally elsewhere. Other songs were brought into either the Ozarks or Appalachia from elsewhere and are not found in both regions. The song "La Guignolée," about a New Year's Eve tradition formerly practiced in French communities in America, seems not to be known traditionally in Appalachia. Here is one text from the Missouri Ozarks:

Bons'r le maître et la maîtresse, y'etent le bonne du logis.
Pour le dernier jour d'l'année, c'était la guignolée vous vous
duevez
Si vous voulez rien nous donnez, dite nous le, (bis)
On vous demande seulement une échinée.
Une échinée n'est pas grand chose, aux deux quatre-vingt-dix
pieds de long. (bis)
Va-t-aller dire à ma maîtresse qu'alle ait toujours,
Qu'elle ait toujours le coeur joyeux, point de tristesse.
Toutes les figures qui ont point d'amant, comment vieillent eilles?
C'est les amours qui la reveillent, hon que l'empêchent de
dormir. (bis)
Quand on arrive au milieu du bois, no fumes à l'ombre.
J'ai attendu le cou-cou chanter, c'est la colombe.
On te fera faire bonne chaire; on te fera chauffer les pieds. (bis)[32]

Good night to the master and mistress, and to all the people of
the household!
For the first day of the year you owe us the Guignolée.
If you have nothing to give us, say so.
We do not ask you to give us much, only a chine of pork ninety
feet long, 'tis no great thing.
Again we do not ask for much, only the eldest daughter of the
house; we will feast her and keep her feet well warmed.
Let us dance the rag dance, let us dance the rag dance so.
Good night to the master and mistress of the household.[33]

There are also some differences musically between Appalachian and Ozark folksongs, the most significant being that the Ozark song is less likely to have minors or minor sounds. This may have been more evident in years past than it is now, but it does seem to be a tradition of relatively long standing. Many Ozark singers, of course, have always used minors and minor sounds, but when given a choice the Ozark singer is much more likely than the Appalachian folksinger to omit them.

What about the people who sing the songs? It may seem odd to stress that it is various human beings who keep the songs alive by singing them. Yet until fairly recently, most folksong and ballad texts were presented as though they existed superorganically, without the aid of people. Even now, most collections of traditional songs give little more about the informant than the name and date of collection. One weakness of the present volume is that I was not always able to obtain extensive data on informants. Whatever was available is given in the notes that follow each entry.

Just who are the singers who maintain the folksong tradition? What type of person takes on this responsibility? The answer is that many different kinds of people are folksong singers. In a few cases folksingers are rustic, uneducated illiterates—just as they are stereotypically pictured. But in the vast majority of instances, this view is wrong. Also erroneous is the notion that folksingers are poor, left-of-center politically, and spend their time singing protest material. Again, there are some folksingers like that—but many others who are not. Actually, a folksinger is an intelligent person— from either a rural or urban background, of any economic or educational background, and of any political inclination—who has enough interest in folksongs to sing them and a good enough memory to recall them.

There are many people with intelligence and good memories who have an interest in folksongs and ballads but simply aren't good singers of traditional songs. They are what the Swedish folklorist Carl Wilhelm von Sydow labeled "passive bearers" of tradition. Unlike active tradition bearers, "the passive bearers have indeed heard of what a certain tradition contains, and may perhaps when questioned, recollect part of it, but do nothing themselves to spread it or keep it alive." Passive bearers of all types of folk traditions, be they songs or not, play a significant role by providing an audience to reinforce and prolong a tradition. It is, of course, possible for a singer to sit and sing songs to himself, but it is not likely that the songs are going to remain in tradition long if the singer is his sole audience. Passive bearers also act, to some extent, as a means of maintaining songs in their traditional format. If, for example, some change is made in a song, passive singers can easily correct it, "and they do so, which is of great importance for the unchanging survival of the tradition."[34]

A not uncommon situation is for passive and active bearers to change their relationship to folk tradition. Passive bearers might become active for a variety of reasons. For example, if people hear a tradition long enough that they become thoroughly conversant with it and take it actively in hand, then they are no longer passive bearers. On the other hand, active bearers may become passive for a number of reasons. For example, children may know many children's folksongs but become passive concerning them once they have outgrown their childhoods. Usually, though, active and passive ballad singers remain so all their lives.

Where do folksingers, active or passive, perform? What is the environment in which folksongs are sung? The answer is simple: they are performed just about anywhere, although usually before an audience of at least one person besides the singer. True, folksongs can be sung by singers for their own enjoyment when they are by themselves. But generally there is some other audience involved, in most cases a small one. Typically the folksinger has a more intimate relationship and greater interplay with the audience than is the case with either classical or popular musicians—a reflection of folksinging's informal nature.

Granted that traditional singers perform just about anywhere they have an audience, the question remains: why do they sing folksongs? There is no single answer for there are a myriad of reasons, almost as many as there are folksingers. Sometimes singers like the sentiments expressed by the lyrics; in other instances they like the tune. In rare cases performers may like melodies so well that they will utilize them for other songs with which they are not generally associated. My own fieldwork in the Arkansas Ozarks revealed a man with a traditional repertoire of about fifty songs who was so taken with the tune for "Take Me Back to Tulsa" that he also used it for fifteen other songs.

Some singers keep songs alive because they are considered part of their own heritage. This is particularly true when the song was associated with a beloved person close to the singer. Noble Cowden, an excellent traditional singer of ballads and folksongs from Cushman, Arkansas, says that one of the reasons she sings the numbers she does is because most of them were learned from her parents, Albert and Sophronia Bullard, and this association alone makes the songs meaningful to her. She now performs several of the songs mainly because they are liked by her family and frequently requested by them. There are, of course, many other possibilities, but the few mentioned here are sufficient to make the point that there is no single reason explaining why traditional singers perform folksongs.

One other matter concerning folksingers merits consideration, namely, the manner in which they perform. Any active bearer of folklore, musical or otherwise, presents his or her material in a specific manner. Folksingers in Appalachia and the Ozarks, and in many other parts of the United States, perform in an impersonal way that scholars sometimes refer to as an "objective" style. They maintain one tempo, one level of intensity, one timbre throughout a song. They remain, in a sense, detached from the lyrics and do not resort to any intrusions that detract from the song. The lyrics provide the mood and the sentiments expressed; all else is secondary. There is certainly no employing of musical dynamics, such as the art or popular singer uses, to spotlight important points in a song. The part of "Prisoner's Song" about being "carried to the new jail tomorrow" most likely would be treated by the art singer as a very significant point calling for the use of such musical dynamics as diminuendos (lowering of volume), crescendos (increasing volume), or ritardandos (slowing down), to emphasize its importance. Folksingers, however, treat these lyrics no differently than any other in the song.

Finally, we should examine the six categories used in this book. Songs about love and lovers is the largest section, reflecting the fact that there are more traditional songs on this topic than on any other in Appalachian and Ozark repertoires. Probably the second most popular category of folksongs in the two regions is religious songs. Children's songs are not necessarily just sung by children, although that often is the case. Many such songs are also found in adult repertoires—performed mostly for children but occasionally for other adults as well. Songs for social occasions includes mainly songs associated with play-parties, dances, and drinking songs; but, of course, there are many other social occasions at which songs might be sung. Some collectors have given such emphasis to songs of work that many people may feel it is the most important category of Southern mountain folksongs. They may also envision happy mountaineers blissfully singing anytime they have to work. Both views are misleading. Not every worker sings, or even feels like singing, while performing his or her daily tasks. And, whether judged on the basis of sheer numbers or overall popularity, work songs are far from being the most important type of Southern mountain folksongs—which is not to say they are insignificant in the Ozarks and Appalachians. Finally, I think the label comic songs is self-explanatory.

The various songs given under each category represent only some of those known traditionally in Appalachia or the Ozarks, and they are not necessarily even the most popular examples of the six types, though many of them would appear in any list of the most popular Southern mountain folksongs. They should be regarded merely as representative selections.

In an earlier book on ballads, I made the following statement: "I am fully aware that arranging the ballads by textual considerations tends to ignore the importance of ballad music, but in my defense I offer the argument that it is the method most often used by editors of ballad collections and therefore has tradition on its side."[35] If *folksong* is substituted for *ballad,* the same statement applies to this book, and I offer the same defense. Music, however, has not been totally ignored, and I have included the melody transcriptions for each song. In a few cases I also have provided melody lines for more than one text of a song or for related songs. The accompanying headnotes provide historical information on each song.

Most writers and editors conclude their work with a sense of relief that their manuscript is finally completed and a wish that the volume they have produced will prove useful to many readers. The present editor is guilty on both counts. I hope that *Southern Mountain Folksongs* will find its way into many libraries, and that a large number of people will read, enjoy, and—if they wish—sing the book's songs. My greatest hope, though, is that readers will take this work as convincing evidence that folksinging not only is alive in Appalachia and the Ozarks, but is flourishing there.

—*W.K. McNeil*
THE OZARK FOLK CENTER
MOUNTAIN VIEW, ARKANSAS

NOTES

1. In this introduction, the word *Appalachia* refers to southern Appalachia unless otherwise stated.

2. In *Buying the Wind: Regional Folklore in the United States* (Chicago: The University of Chicago Press, 1964), 166, Richard M. Dorson clearly suggests that the Ozarks and Appalachia are, from a folklore viewpoint, mirror images. Many other examples could be cited.

3. For a more detailed discussion of these points, see my book *The Charm Is Broken: Readings in Arkansas and Missouri Folklore* (Little Rock: August House, 1984), 11-13.

4. For varying views on the boundaries of southern Appalachia, see John C. Campbell, *The Southern Highlander and His Homeland* (1921; reprint, Lexington: The University Press of Kentucky, 1969), 10-18; Rupert B. Vance, "The Region: A New Survey," in *The Southern Appalachian Region: A Survey* ed. Thomas R. Ford (1962; reprint, Lexington: The University of Kentucky Press, 1967), 3; Jack E. Weller, *Yesterday's People: Life in Contemporary Appalachia* (Lexington: The University of Kentucky Press, 1966), 9; and W.D. Weatherford and Earl D.C. Brewer, *Life and Religion in Southern Appalachia* (New York: Friendship Press, 1962). For a similar discussion of the various boundaries of the Ozarks, see my book *Ozark Mountain Humor: Jokes on Hunting, Religion, Marriage and Ozark Ways* (Little Rock: August House, 1989), 11.

5. W.K. McNeil, *Appalachian Images in Folk and Popular Culture* (Ann Arbor, Michigan: UMI Research Press, 1989), 1-2.

6. For a discussion of these, see my *Ozark Mountain Humor*, 11-13.

7. Milton D. Rafferty, *The Ozarks: Land and Life* (Norman: University of Oklahoma Press, 1980), 6.

8. Collected in 1979 by W.K. McNeil from Kenneth Rorie, Batesville, Arkansas. Rorie can be heard singing the song on *Not Far From Here ... Traditional Tales and Songs Recorded in the Arkansas Ozarks*. Arkansas Traditions, no number.

9. Collected in 1979 by W.K. McNeil from Noble Cowden, Cushman, Arkansas. Cowden can be heard singing the song on *Not Far From Here.*

10. *The Frank C. Brown Collection of North Carolina Folklore* (Durham: Duke University Press, 1952), III, 280-81. The text was collected in 1922 from I.G. Greer, Boone, North Carolina.

11. Collected in 1979 by W.K. McNeil from Noble Cowden. She can be heard singing the song on *Not Far From Here.*

12. Text quoted from Roger D. Abrahams and George Foss, *Anglo-American Folksong Style* (Englewood Cliffs, New Jersey: Prentice-Hall, 1968), 40-41. Despite the title of their book, the Abrahams-Foss volume is primarily concerned with Anglo-American balladry.

13. Shenstone is quoted in volume III of the *The Frank C. Brown Collection of North Carolina Folklore*, 3.

14. See Brown III, 275 and Celeste P. Cambiaire, *East Tennessee and Western Virginia Mountain Ballads* (London: The Mitre Press, 1935), 37.

15. Francis J. Child, *The English and Scottish Popular Ballads* (1882; reprint, New York: Dover Publications, 1965), I, vii.

16. Richard Chase, *American Folk Tales and Songs* (New York: The New American Library of World Literature, 1956), 229.

17. Child, *English and Scottish Popular Ballads*, I, Advertisement to Part I, vii.

18. Brown, III, 3.

19. Tristram P. Coffin, "A Tentative Study of a Typical Folk Lyric: 'Green Grows the Laurel.'" *Journal of American Folklore*, 65:258 (October-December, 1952): 341-51.

20. Ibid., 341.

21. Judith Marie McCulloh, "'In the Pines': The Melodic-Textual Identity of an American Lyric Folksong Cluster." Ph. D. diss., Indiana University, 1970.

22. Brown, II, 161. The text was collected by Maude Minish Sutton from the singing of "Aunt Becky" Gordon of Stateline Hill, Henderson County, North Carolina.

23. Ibid., 713. Titled "Tom Dula's Lament," this was from the singing of Maude Minish Sutton, Lenoir, North Carolina.

24. W.C. Handy, *Father of the Blues*, ed. Arna Bontemps (1941; reprint, New York: Collier Books, 1970), 153.

25. D.K. Wilgus and Eleanor R. Long, "The *Blues Ballad* and the Genesis of Style in Traditional Narrative Song," in *Narrative Folksong: New Directions* ed. Carol L. Edwards and Kathleen E.B. Manley (Boulder, Colorado: Westview Press, 1985), 443.

26. Ibid., 440-41.

27. Coffin, "'Green Grows the Laurel,'" 341.

28. Vance Randolph, *Ozark Folksongs* (1946-1950; reprint, Columbia: University of Missouri Press, 1980), I, 116. Randolph collected the song March 6, 1927, from Louise Long, Rocky Comfort, Missouri.

29. Brown, III, 287-88. The song was collected in August 1937 from Frank Proffitt, Sugar Grove, North Carolina.

30. Collected by W.K. McNeil from the Williams Family, Roland, Arkansas, April 1986. The Williams Family can be heard singing the song on *All in the Family*. Arkansas Traditions 004.

31. Collected by W.K. McNeil from the Williams Family, Roland, Arkansas, April 1986. The Williams Family can be heard singing the song on *All in the Family*.

32. Collected from Rose Pratt, Old Mines, Missouri, in 1977 by unidentified fieldworkers for the Missouri Friends of the Folk Arts. Pratt can be heard singing the song on *I'm Old But I'm Awfully Tough: Traditional Music of the Ozark Region*. MFFA 1001.

33. The translation is from Wilson Primm, "New Year's Day in the Olden Time of St. Louis," *Missouri Historical Society Journal* (Jan. 1900): 15, and also is found in the booklet accompanying *I'm Old But I'm Awfully Tough*.

34. C.W. von Sydow, *Selected Papers of Folklore* (1948; reprint, New York: Arno Press, 1977), 12-14.

35. W.K. McNeil, *Southern Folk Ballads*, 2 volumes (Little Rock: August House, 1987-1988), 29.

Songs about Love and Lovers

Little Birdie

This piece is related to "I Wish I Were Single Again" (a connection more obvious in several other published versions than in the one given here), but it is really a different song of unknown origin. Leonard Roberts suggests it is derived from a nineteenth-century song titled "A Married Woman's Lament." The lyrics are presented here so that readers may judge for themselves just how close this piece is to "Little Birdie":

A Married Woman's Lament

Oh Cupid, oh Cupid, you use me severe,
You kept me a-loving for seven long years.
You kept me a-loving in anguish and pain,
Oh, how I wish I was single again.

Before I was married, 'twas nothing but love,
'Twas, Oh my ducky darling, my sweet honey dove,
But now I am married, it's quite a different thing,
Get up and get the breakfast, you darn lazy thing.

Before I was married, I lived at my ease,
But now I am married, I have a husband to please,
Four small children and them to maintain,
Oh, how I wish I was single again!

Washing and mending, we daily have to do,
Ironing and baking must be remembered too,
House to clean up when spring comes, too,
The young ones are squalling, oh, what will I do?

One cries, "Mother, I want a piece of bread,"
The other cries, "Mama, I want to go to bed."
Take those children and put them to bed,
Before their Father curses them, and wishes they were dead.

If "Little Birdie" is based on this song, the connection is solely textual, for the melody and meter are different in the two pieces.

Whatever the origin of "Little Birdie," it is undeniable that commercial recordings have played a part in popularizing the song. One of the most important of these was made for the Columbia label in the 1920s by Marion Try Slaughter under the name Al Craver. Slaughter (1883–1948) was one of the most popular and prolific country artists of the era—so prolific that he used literally dozens of pseudonyms, of which the best known was Vernon Dalhart.

Slaughter was a trained singer who began his professional career as a performer of light opera, and for that reason his work is often dismissed as of little importance to students of old-time country music and folk music. Even so, he had a fully traditional background, one that was more folk than that of other commercial country musicians who always have been accepted by scholars as traditional. As for Slaughter's importance to folk music specialists, one has only to leaf through the pages of folksong collections to find evidence of his influence. The version of "Little Birdie" included by Leonard Roberts in *In the Pine* is very close to Slaughter's 1920s recording. Of course, other country artists also performed the song, including an all-girl string band, The Coon Creek Girls. More recently, Ralph Stanley and the Clinch Mountain Boys have kept it alive on the bluegrass circuit.

The present text of "Little Birdie" is from the singing of Lily May Ledford, Berea, Kentucky. It was one of several songs she performed in a concert at Berea College, June 25, 1975. Ledford (1917-1985) was a long-time member of The Coon Creek Girls;

indeed, she was one of the band's originals, performing regularly with them from 1937 to 1957 and sporadically thereafter.

In 1936, Lily May entered a contest near her home in Powell County in eastern Kentucky. Her first prize included a contract to play on the radio in Chicago. She appeared on a daily program and on the Saturday night WLS National Barn Dance, the most important country music show of the day. In 1937 she and her sister Rosie, who had joined her in Chicago, moved to Cincinnati station WLW, where The Coon Creek Girls were formed. Two years later, the band went to Renfro Valley, Kentucky, where John Lair (who formed and named The Coon Creek Girls) started holding the Renfro Valley Barn Dance. Although there were several personnel changes, the band remained in Renfro Valley throughout the remainder of its existence.

Lily May and The Coon Creek Girls were professional country musicians, but much of their repertoire was traditional, often known by the Ledford women from their own family. John Lair, who was an authority on folk music, also gave them many songs and often helped them with their arrangements. Apparently, Lily May learned "Little Birdie" from members of her family.

Little Birdie

RECORDED FROM THE SINGING OF LILY MAY LEDFORD IN BEREA, KENTUCKY, JUNE 25, 1975. MUSIC TRANSCRIPTION BY DAN BRACKIN. LYRIC TRANSCRIPTION BY W.K. McNEIL.

Little birdie, little birdie,
What makes you fly so high?
It's because I have a true love,
I don't have to die,
Oh, I don't have to die.

Little birdie, little birdie,
What makes you seem so blue?
It's nothing else but trouble,
A-grieving over you,
Oh, a-grieving over you.

Little woman, pretty woman,
What makes you act so down?
You ain't got no right to worry,
You ain't got no right to frown,
Oh, no right to frown.

Little birdie, little birdie,
Won't you sing to me your song?
Just a short time to stay here
And a long time to be gone,
Oh, a long time to be gone.

Prisoner's Song / Tragic Romance

This song created a great sensation in 1924 when it was recorded by Marion Try Slaughter under the pseudonym of Vernon Dalhart as one-half of Victor record number 19427. Up to that time Slaughter was known mainly as a singer of light opera and pop songs like "Can't Yo' Heah Me Callin' Caroline?" After the Victor record was released, he focused his attentions on singing country music.

The reason was simple: Slaughter's rendition of "Prisoner's Song" was the biggest-selling vocal record ever made up to that time. Its great success undoubtedly accounts for the large number of conflicting stories (some of them started by Slaughter himself) about the song's origin. The most-often-repeated tale was that Slaughter's cousin, Guy Massey, wrote the song. Slaughter sometimes said *he* wrote it to fill the reverse side of a record. Nathaniel Shilkret, Victor's musical director at the time, insisted that Slaughter brought in a few "pencilled notes but no music" that Shilkret told him "couldn't be used as it stood, but...might be fixed up to do." According to this story, Shilkret then took Slaughter's manuscript home and "wrote more verses and ground out a simple, mournful tune to fit the words." He then submitted the finished work to Slaughter, who was "well pleased."

In the 1970s, Novie Massey, the wife of one of Slaughter's cousins, provided yet another account of the song's origin. To Dorothy Horstman, the author of *Sing Your Heart Out, Country Boy,* a book purporting to tell the "true" stories behind several classic country songs, Mrs. Massey alleged that her husband wrote the song:

> Guy Massey did not write this song. His brother, Robert Massey, wrote it. Guy always stayed with us when he came to Dallas, and I was with them while my husband sang it and Guy wrote it down. He said he wanted to take it to New York. Well, he did, and he copyrighted it in his own name. Up until the time we were married, Robert traveled around over the country, and he picked up part of it somewhere and put words to it. He was singing it when we were

married in 1920. Guy tried to put it on record, but he failed, then their cousin, Vernon Dalhart, recorded it, and it just went like wildfire. In his will, Guy willed it back to my husband, but he never did admit that he didn't write it.

Actually, none of these claims is true, for the piece was a folksong that predated the 1920s by decades. Because the history of this song is very complex and involves a merging of items from several others, it is impossible to say just how far back before 1924 it goes. But it is safe to say that some elements of the song predate the Slaughter recording by almost a century. Sometime before 1840, Charles Jefferys, a popular lyricist of the day, wrote "Oh! Had I the Wings of a Dove" that was set to music by one L. Devereaux. This song opens with the following lines:

> *Oh! had I wings like a dove, I would fly*
> *Away from this world of care;*
> *My soul would mount to the realms on high*
> *And seek a refuge there.*

If the number of printings is an accurate indication, this song was quite popular throughout the nineteenth century. In 1842 the words were printed without music in *The Souvenir Minstrel or Singer's Remember Me,* and both lyrics and music appeared in William Oakes's *Sabbath Evenings* (1840), Isaac Baker Woodbury's *Lute of Zion* (1856), Oliver Ditson's *Continental Harmony* (1857), in numerous sheet music and song collection editions issued between 1870 and 1900, and in the *Musical Bouquet* series published in London. It also was performed on numerous occasions by the Hutchinson Family of New Hampshire, one of America's most popular singing groups in the antebellum years.

About 1850 there appeared an English broadside ballad titled "Farewell to All Judges and Juries" or "Farewell to Judges and Juries" (it is reported both ways) that concludes with the following lines:

How often I wish that the eagle
Would lend me her wings, I would fly;
Then I'd fly to the arms of my Polly,
And on her soft bosom, I'd die.

This ballad was later parodied in a music hall piece titled "Botany Bay" or "Seven Long Years in Prison" that was introduced by David Belasco Jones in the 1885 musical comedy *Little Jack Shepherd*. It became very popular not only in England but also in Australia, after the musical comedy in which it appeared was produced in Melbourne in 1886. Eventually its appeal spread to the United States—proof of its popularity being that the melody was borrowed for a college nonsense song, "If I Had the Wings of a Caterpillar."

In 1826 Joseph Augustus or—in some sources—Augustine Wade (1800-1875) wrote a song titled either "Meet Me in the Moonlight Alone" or "Meet Me By Moonlight Alone" (sources list it both ways). Several folklorists believe the Wade piece is merely a version of "Prisoner's Song," but the connection between the two is thin. The only similarity is in the ardent bid for a meeting, set forth in the opening lines:

Meet me by moonlight alone,
And then I will tell you a tale;
Must be told by the moonlight alone,
In the grove at the end of the vale.

The song contains no mention of wings, ships, or prisons, but instead consists of lines like the following:

Daylight may do for the gay,
The thoughtless, the heartless, the free,
But there's something about the moon's ray
That is sweeter to you and to me.

Sometime soon after the Civil War, an American broadside ballad titled "There's a Fine Ship on the Ocean" appeared. As far as is now known, its first publication was by Henry J. Wehman between 1880 and 1886. The ship and eagle's wings motifs and the meeting by moonlight verses are included in this song, but it lacks a reference to prisons or prisoners.

Yet another song of unknown origin plays a role in the history of "Prisoner's Song." Despite its similarity in title to Wade's 1826 piece, "Meet Me in the Moonlight" is a different song. It existed by the 1880s, for in 1924 Vance Randolph collected a version from Mrs. Carrie Baber, Pineville, Missouri, who claimed to have heard the song in 1889. Carl Sandburg also reported hearing it in 1898. Even so, there is no extant text collected prior to the twentieth century. The earliest-known one, contributed in 1914 to Frank C. Brown by Amy Henderson of Worry, North Carolina, bears strong resemblance to the "Prisoner's Song" recorded in 1924 by Slaughter. For sake of comparison, both are offered here—the Henderson text first, then the Slaughter version:

Meet Me in the Moonlight

Off to the jail house tomorrow
Not far to leave my little darling alone,
With them cold iron bars around me
And my pillow is made of stone.

CHORUS:
Meet me tonight, darling, meet me
Out in the moonlight alone,
For I have a secret to tell you
Must be told in the moonlight alone.

Oh, I heard that your parents don't like me,
They have driven me away from their door;
If I had those days to go over
I would never come back any more.

If I had a ship on the ocean
All lined with bright silver and gold,
Before my darling should suffer
My ship should be anchored and sold.

I am dying for someone to love me
And someone to call me their own,
For someone to be with me always;
I am tired of living alone.

The Prisoner's Song

Oh, I wish I had someone to love me,
Someone to call me their own;
Oh, I wish I had someone to live with,
'Cause I'm tired of livin' alone.

Oh, please meet me tonight in the moonlight,
Please meet me tonight all alone;
For I have a sad story to tell you,
It's a story that's never been told.

I'll be carried to the new jail tomorrow,
Leaving my poor darling alone;
With the cold prison bars all around me,
And my head on a pillow of stone.

Now I have a grand ship on the ocean,
All mounted with silver and gold;
And before my poor darlin' would suffer,
Oh, that ship would be anchored and sold.

Now if I had the wings of an angel,
Over these prison walls I would fly;
And I'd fly to the arms of my poor darlin',
And there I'd be willing to die.

Sorting out the genealogy of the tune is every bit as complicated as determining the ancestry of the lyrics. Many speculations that have been offered do not hold up under scrutiny. In *A History of Popular Music in America*, Sigmund Spaeth suggests that there are "slight echoes" of Henry Clay Work's 1865 pop melody, "The Ship That Never Returned," in "Prisoner's Song." In an earlier book, *Weep Some More, My Lady*, Spaeth is more positive in asserting the "melody of the verse strongly suggests that of the modern

'Prisoner's Song.'" Carl Sandburg agreed with Spaeth in this regard, but the claim put forth by the two men is unconvincing because the melodies show no relationship other than what might be accounted for by mere coincidence.

In *American Mountain Songs,* Ethel Park Richardson finds suggestions of "The Prisoner's Song" melody in an 1897 popular piece, "The Letter Edged in Black"; but here, too, the argument is a weak one that is not generally accepted. Some versions of "Prisoner's Song"—for example the one in Cazden, Haufrecht, and Studer, p. 375—do feature the melody of the nineteenth-century song "Red River Valley," but that is not the tune most often heard. Neither "Farewell to Judges and Juries" nor the Wade song from 1826 bears any strong resemblance to the most commonly used melody. This leaves the broadside ballad "There's a Fine Ship on the Ocean" and the anonymous composition "Meet Me in the Moonlight" as the most likely melodic sources of "Prisoner's Song." There is, of course, the added possibility that Nathaniel Shilkret is largely responsible for the melody generally used today.

So it seems likely, as Walter D. Haden suggests in two articles on Slaughter published in the *John Edwards Memorial Foundation Quarterly,* that either Guy or Bob Massey learned the song in their youth and taught it to Slaughter. In any case, they certainly had nothing to do with writing the song, which is derived from a blending of several nineteenth-century numbers. In folksong collections many titles are reported, including "Meet Me in the Moonlight," "Prisoner Walls," "Sweet Lulur," "I Have a Ship on the Ocean," "I Had a Little Ship," "New Jail," and "Meet Me Tonight," among others. While the song certainly was popular prior to 1924, there can be little doubt that the Slaughter record increased its popularity. Probably, this is also the reason most traditional versions now focus on the motifs of the jail, the moonlight, and a ship.

The present version was recorded January 23, 1979, by John Hershberger in Richmond, Kentucky, from the singing of Earl Barnes and his sons Randy and Danny. Other than the information that Barnes was locally noted for his singing, no data is provided about him.

Prisoner's Song (Tragic Romance)

COLLECTED BY JOHN HERSHBERGER FROM EARL, RANDY, AND DANNY BARNES, RICHMOND, KENTUCKY, JANUARY 23, 1979. MUSIC TRANSCRIPTION BY DAN BRACKIN. LYRIC TRANSCRIPTION BY W.K. McNEIL.

Well, I wish I had someone to love me,
I had someone to call me "my own."
And I wish I had someone to live with,
For I'm tired of living alone.

I said meet me tonight, darling meet me,
Meet me out in the moonlight alone.
For I have a sad story to tell,
Must be told in the moonlight alone.

I'll be carried to the new jail tomorrow,
Leaving my poor darling alone,
With them cold prison bars all around me
And my head on a pillow of stone.

I said meet me tonight, darling meet me,
Meet me out in the moonlight alone.
For I have a sad story to tell,
Must be told in the moonlight alone.

I have a great ship on the ocean,
All lined with silver and gold;
And before my poor darling shall suffer
That ship would be anchored and sold.

I said meet me tonight, darling meet me,
Meet me out in the moonlight alone.
For I have a sad story to tell,
Must be told in the moonlight alone.

Pig in a Pen / Going to Little Creek

This folksong, two versions of which appear next, is made up primarily of phrases found in other songs, most notably "Liza Jane," "Cindy," and "Sally Goodin'." Some versions also contain lines usually associated with "Shady Grove." Because these lyrics are found in so many songs, it is all but impossible to date this specific arrangement of them. The best one can do is note that the two forms given here definitely were entrenched in the folksong tradition of Appalachia and the Ozarks by the early twentieth century. How much before that time they were around is open to speculation; certainly some of the individual elements existed by the mid-nineteenth century, and possibly before. The most widespread is the needle-and-thread motif which appears in many songs of minstrel, or presumed minstrel-show, origin. Only slightly less traveled is the pig-in-a-pen stanza. The finger ring motif and the lines about blessing the coffee pot and spout are the other most common elements in versions of this song.

The "Pig in a Pen" form usually has only the one title, but the other version given here has a place name in the title that changes depending on where the song was learned or the community the singer believes it refers to. According to its singer, the song presented here was named for an eastern Kentucky community. But Bascom Lamar Lunsford sang a version of it called "Italy" or "Going to Italy" after a North Carolina mountain community of that name.

Undoubtedly, commercial influences have boosted the popularity of the song, especially the "Pig in a Pen" form. As this book's discography shows, the piece has been recorded several times, the most influential of these being a February 17, 1937, effort by Fiddlin' Arthur Smith. Because textually Smith's recording differs considerably from most versions reported in folksong collections, it is given here:

Got that pig at home in a pen,
Corn to feed him on.
All I need's a pretty little girl
To feed him when I'm gone.

Went to see my darlin',
What do you think she said?
She said she would not marry me
If the rest of the boys were dead.

Got that pig at home in a pen,
Corn to feed him on.
All I need's a pretty little girl
To feed him when I'm gone.

When she saw me comin'
She wrung her hands and cried,
"Yonder comes the sweetest boy
That ever lived or died."

When she saw me leavin'
She wrung her hands and cried,
"Yonder goes the meanest boy
That ever lived or died."

Got that pig at home in a pen,
Corn to feed him on.
All I need's a pretty little girl
To feed him when I'm gone.

Arthur Smith (1898–1971) was a native of Humphreys County, Tennessee, who became a legendary country musician. He was among the earliest performers on the Grand Ole Opry, first appearing in 1927 as a solo fiddler. Later he teamed with a cousin, Homer Smith, and they appeared for four years, during which time they were often erroneously billed as the "Smith Brothers." Then Arthur teamed up with Sam and Kirk McGee as the Dixieliners (after the N.C. and St. L. Railroad, known in middle Tennessee as the Dixie Line). This group became one of the most popular string bands of the 1930s.

Smith also performed with the Delmore Brothers (Alton and Rabon) as the Arthur Smith Trio. They made a number of successful recordings—many of them, like "There's More Pretty Girls Than One" and "Beautiful Brown Eyes," derived from the folk tradition of the South and later influencing that same tradition. In the 1940s Smith played with a number of bands including the Bailes Brothers and Jimmy Wakely. Then he drifted out of music for some years but, like many other early country musicians, was "rediscovered" in the so-called folk revival of the 1960s. During that decade Smith frequently performed with and made several albums with the McGee Brothers.

The text of "Pig in a Pen" given here was recorded in Berea, Kentucky, by Loyal Jones, on July 2, 1974, from the singing of George Pegram and Walter "Red" Parham. Pegram, who died shortly after this song was taped, started playing in 1921 on a cigar box banjo he made. Some musical rudiments he picked up from an uncle, but basically his musical knowledge came from listening to other musicians. For many years he worked for the Southern Railroad as an entertainer at their meetings, held all over the United States. He made several records, mostly with Parham, a farmer and construction worker to whom he'd been introduced by Bascom Lamar Lunsford in 1949. Parham played guitar and harmonica in addition to singing, and for a brief period he was a regular performer at Ghost Town, a tourist attraction in Maggie Valley, North Carolina. Parham was very well known for his unusual and entertaining method of playing the harmonica. He held the instrument back in his mouth between his cheek and teeth, rolled it in and out, and sang around it, at the same time accompanying himself on the guitar. For many years Parham and Pegram performed together at festivals and fiddle conventions. They were crowd-pleasing favorites at Lunsford's Mountain Dance and Folk Festival in Asheville, North Carolina, the state where both lived.

"Going to Little Creek" is from the singing of Doc Hopkins and is taken off a tape he made in the late 1960s. He learned the song, which he believed was about a community in the Cumberland Mountains, during his youth in Harlan County, Kentucky. For more information on Hopkins, see the notes for "Pretty Little Pink."

Pig in a Pen

COLLECTED BY LOYAL JONES FROM GEORGE PEGRAM AND WALTER "RED" PARHAM IN BEREA, KENTUCKY, JULY 2, 1974. MUSIC TRANSCRIPTION BY DAN BRACKIN. LYRIC TRANSCRIPTION BY W.K. McNEIL.

I gotta hog and a pig in the pen,
Corn to feed him on,
All I want's a pretty little gal,
Feed him when I'm gone,
Feed him when I'm gone.

If I had a needle and thread
As fine as I could sew,
I'd sew my true love to my side
And down the road I'd go.

I gotta hog and a pig in the pen,
Corn to feed him on,
All I want's a pretty little gal,
Feed him when I'm gone.

God bless the coffee pot,
God bless the spout,
God bless the pretty little girl
That pours my coffee out.

I gotta hog and a pig in the pen,
Corn to feed him on,
All I want's a pretty little gal,
Feed him when I'm gone.

Going to Little Creek

FROM THE SINGING OF DOC HOPKINS. MUSIC AND LYRIC TRANSCRIPTIONS
BY DAN BRACKIN.

Yonder comes-a my true love
How do you reckon I know?
Know her by her golden curls
Hangin' down so low.

Goin' to Little Creek, little 'fore long,
Goin' to Little Creek, little 'fore long,
Goin' to Little Creek, little 'fore long,
See that gal of mine.

It's finger ring, it's finger ring,
Shines so bright like gold,
I'm a-goin' to marry that pretty little girl
Before she gets too old.

Goin' to Little Creek a little 'fore long,
Goin' to Little Creek a little 'fore long,
Goin' to Little Creek a little 'fore long,
See that gal of mine.

Banjo Pickin' Girl

This song is relatively well known in Southern mountain folk tradition, but to my knowledge it appears in no other folksong publication from the Appalachians or the Ozarks, probably because of the piece's strong commercial ties. Also known as "Going Around the World," it probably predates the twentieth century; but thus far, no text has been reported from before 1900. Patricia Hall and Charles Wolfe in their notes for the album *Banjo Pickin' Girl* make the statement that "parts of this song have been traced to the middle of the sixteenth century." Although Hall and Wolfe do not provide examples or say which parts they had in mind, there is no reason to quibble with the comment. It is, indeed, quite likely that one can trace individual stanzas of a song made up of "floating verses" back to an ancient past. It is also fair to say that while the song consists of various elements that may have an ancestry dating back several centuries, in the form known today it is very much of the twentieth century.

One possible ancestor mentioned by Hall and Wolfe is the 1878 song "Baby Mine" by Charles Mackay or Mackey (it is spelled both ways in reference sources) and Harrison Millard, who used the pseudonym Archibald Johnston. This number, popularized by Belle Cole, a very successful singer of the day, contained a melody later appropriated for the Illinois state song and was also echoed in Raymon Moore's 1893 pop song "Sweet Marie." If "Banjo Pickin' Girl" is derived from this source, then the melody has undergone considerable transformation and the lyrics have changed even more dramatically. All this will be evident to readers who compare the text presented later with the Mackay-Millar song given here:

Baby Mine

LYRICS BY CHARLES MACKAY, OR MACKEY. MUSIC BY HARRISON MILLARD.

I've a letter from thy sire, Baby mine;
I could read and never tire, Baby mine;
He is sailing o'er the sea,
He is coming home to me,
He is coming back to thee! Baby mine! Baby mine;
He is coming back to thee! Baby mine.

Oh, I long to see his face, Baby mine, Baby mine;
In his old accustomed place, Baby mine;
Like the rose of May in bloom,
Like a star amid the gloom,
Like the sunshine in the room, Baby mine! Baby mine;
Like the sunshine in the room, Baby mine.

I'm so glad, I cannot sleep, Baby mine, Baby mine;
I'm so happy, I would weep, Baby mine, Baby mine;
He is sailing o'er the sea,
He is coming home to me,
He is coming back to thee! Baby mine! Baby mine,
He is coming back to thee! Baby mine.

A stronger connection is found in the work of Dick Burnett, a blind musician from Monticello, Kentucky. Richard Daniel Burnett (1883-1977) became a professional country musician out of necessity after a vicious assault by a robber left him blind and without any other means of supporting his family. After 1907, when the robbery occurred, Burnett traveled to towns throughout south-central Kentucky to sing at fairs, courthouses, train stations, street corners, and any other places where he could draw a crowd. Some would drop money in a tin cup tied to his leg, while others might purchase a small book of his songs or one of his "ballet cards"—small cards containing the words of a song. One of the cards contained the lyrics for "Going Around the World," a song Burnett said he wrote:

> *I'm going across the ocean friend of mine,*
> *I'm going across the ocean friend of mine*
> *I'm going across the ocean if I don't change my notion.*
> *I'm going around the world friend of mine.*
>
> *I'll write my girl a letter friend of mine*
> *I'll write my girl a letter friend of mine*
> *I'll write my girl a letter friend of mine and*
> *I'll write my girl a letter and I'll tell her that she'd better*
> *For I'm going around the world friend of mine.*
>
> *Oh! Come and sit by me girl o' mine*
> *Come and sit down by me girl o' mine.*
> *Come and sit down by me, say you love no one but me,*
> *And we'll go around the world, girl o' mine.*
>
> *Oh, give to me your hand girl o' mine,*
> *Oh! give to me your hand girl o' mine,*
> *Oh! give to me your hand,*
> *Say you love no other man.*
> *And we'll go around the world, girl o' mine.*
>
> *I may cross the sea girl of mine.*
> *I may cross the sea girl of mine.*
> *I may cross the sea.*
> *Oh! come and go with me.*
> *I'm going around the world girl of mine.*

I'm going around the world friend of mine.
I'm going around the world friend of mine.
I've been around the world, with a banjo picking girl,
I've been around the world friend of mine.

It is significant that Burnett's text, the earliest known of "Banjo Pickin' Girl," does not contain the phrase "Baby mine" (supposedly borrowed from the 1878 pop song) but instead has "friend of mine" and "girl of mine" as recurring phrases. He also uses the phrase "banjo picking girl" only in the last line of the "ballet card" text rather than as a recurring phrase. While it is impossible to determine the exact date of this version, it seems unlikely that it could have been printed before 1907 when Burnett took up music full time, though he certainly could have known it earlier.

That Burnett claimed credit for it does not necessarily mean that he wrote the song. Folk musicians frequently claim as their own work the songs that they sing. For example, I once met a man in a northern Arkansas village who insisted that he wrote a song called "Andrew Barton." Apparently, he had convinced others in his community that he was the song's writer, because several people told me his claim was true. Alas, they would never be swayed by the suggestion that the song predated the twentieth century by many decades and even is included in Francis James Child's ten-volume collection *The English and Scottish Popular Ballads* (1882-1898). All this man had created was his own arrangement of a traditional ballad. This is probably also Burnett's relationship to "Going Around the World."

On January 5, 1929, Burnett recorded "Going Around the World" for the Gennett label. It is certain that this version met with no commercial success because it was not released until it appeared on an LP issued in 1976. But it differs from the "ballet card" text primarily in the way stanzas are ordered. Possibly Burnett's recording represents the way he usually sang the song in various towns across eastern Kentucky. For that reason it is given here:

I'm going across the ocean friend of mine.
I'm going across the ocean friend of mine.
I'm going across the ocean if I don't change my notion.
I'm going around the world friend of mine.

Oh! Come and sit by me girl o' mine.
Come and sit down by me girl o' mine.
Come and sit down by me, say you love no one but me,
And we'll go around this world girl o' mine.

Oh, give to me your hand girl o' mine,
Oh, give to me your hand girl o' mine,
Oh, give to me your hand,
Say you love no other man,
And we'll go around this world, girl o' mine.

Oh, Come and sit by me girl o' mine,
Come and sit down by me girl o' mine.
Come and sit down by me, say you love no one but me,
And we'll go around this world girl o' mine.

I'm going around this world friend of mine,
I'm going around this world friend of mine.
I've been around this world with a banjo picking girl,
I've been around this world friend of mine.

Oh, give to me your hand girl o' mine,
Oh, give to me your hand girl o' mine,
Oh, give to me your hand,
Say you love no other man,
And we'll go around this world, girl o' mine.

I may cross the sea girl of mine,
I may cross the sea girl of mine.
I may cross the sea,
Oh, come and go with me,
I'll go around this world girl of mine.

> *I'm going around this world friend of mine,*
> *I'm going around this world friend of mine.*
> *I've been around this world with a banjo picking girl,*
> *I've been around this world friend of mine.*
>
> *I'll write my girl a letter friend of mine,*
> *I'll write my girl a letter friend of mine.*
> *I'll write my girl a letter and I'll tell her that she'd better,*
> *For I'm going around the world friend of mine.*

While Burnett produced what is the earliest extant text of "Banjo Pickin' Girl," another eastern Kentucky singer, Emry Arthur (1900-1966), was the first to make a commercial recording of the song, beating Burnett into the recording studio by seven months. In June 1928, Arthur recorded the song, along with several others, for the Vocalion label. Possibly his text came from Burnett, for the two men were long-time neighbors. In fact, they were born in the same valley, and Arthur and his family and Burnett frequently exchanged songs. But if Burnett was his source, then Arthur altered the song a great deal, slowing down the melody and adding some different lyrics. His text follows:

> *I'm going around this world, baby mine,*
> *I'm going around this world, baby mine.*
> *I'm going around this world,*
> *With a banjo picking girl.*
> *I'm going around this world, baby mine.*
>
> *I'm going across this ocean, baby mine,*
> *I'm going across this ocean, baby mine.*
> *I'm going across this ocean*
> *If I don't change my notion.*
> *I'm going across this ocean, baby mine.*
>
> *I'm going across the sea, baby mine,*
> *I'm going across the sea, baby mine.*
> *I'm going across the sea,*
> *Won't you come and go with me?*
> *I'm going across the sea, baby mine.*

I'm going to Chattanoogie, baby mine,
I'm going to Chattanoogie, baby mine.
I'm going to Chattanoogie,
From there right on to Cuby.
I'm going to Chattanoogie, baby mine.

I'm working by the day, baby mine,
I'm working by the day, baby mine.
I'm working by the day
To get money to pay our way.
I'm working by the day, baby mine.

I'll tell you what I'll do, baby mine,
I'll tell you what I'll do, baby mine,
I'll tell you what I'll do,
I sure will stick to you.
I'll tell you what I'll do, baby mine.

I'm going to write a letter, baby mine,
I'm going to write a letter, baby mine.
I'm going to write a letter
And tell 'em that they'd better.
I'm going to write a letter, baby mine.

After Burnett's unissued 78 of 1929, there were no more commercial recordings of the song until May 30, 1938, when The Coon Creek Girls recorded it in Chicago for the Okeh label. Because that text is essentially the same as the one given here, it is not quoted. This 1938 recording—the most influential of all—is echoed in almost every version heard since, including one collected from Pete Steele for the Library of Congress Archive of Folk Song and one performed by Helen Osborne (who used the stage name Katy Hill) on a radio program in the 1940s.

The text given here was recorded in Berea, Kentucky, January 24, 1980, by Loyal Jones from the singing of Lily May Ledford. (For more information about Ledford, see the notes to "Little Birdie.") About "Banjo Pickin' Girl" Ledford said: "My brother Kelly, who came back from a long stay in Pike County in the nineteen-twenties, brought one verse of this song home. John Lair, Rosie, and I made up more verses and changed it a bit, making it more suitable for a woman." Despite this statement, none of the verses actually originated with the Ledfords or with Lair. All are found in other songs, such as "Roll On, Buddy," so it seems that what the Ledfords and Lair did was to arrange some of a vast stock of "floating verses" in a specific order. It is a thing commonly done by folksingers.

Banjo Pickin' Girl

RECORDED BY LOYAL JONES FROM THE SINGING OF LILY MAY LEDFORD, BEREA, KENTUCKY, JANUARY 24, 1980. MUSIC TRANSCRIPTION BY DAN BRACK-IN. LYRIC TRANSCRIPTION BY W.K. McNEIL.

> I'm goin' around this world, baby mine;
> I'm goin' around this world, baby mine;
> I'm going' around this world,
> I'll be a banjo pickin' girl.
> I'm goin' around this world baby mine.
>
> I'm goin' to Tennessee, baby mine;
> I'm goin' to Tennessee, baby mine;
> I'm goin' to Tennessee,
> Don't you try to follow me.
> I'm goin' to Tennessee, baby mine.
>
> I'm goin' to North Carolina, baby mine;
> I'm goin' to North Carolina, baby mine;
> I'm going to North Carolina,
> And from there on to China.
> I'm goin' to North Carolina, baby mine.

I'm goin' across the ocean, baby mine;
I'm goin' across the ocean, baby mine;
I'm goin' across the ocean,
If I don't change my notion.
I'm goin' across the ocean, baby mine.

Now, if you ain't got no money, baby mine;
If you ain't got no money, baby mine;
If you ain't got no money,
Get yourself another honey.
I'm goin' around this world, baby mine.

Well, I'm goin' around this world, baby mine;
I'm goin' around this world, baby mine;
I'm goin' around this world,
And I'll be a banjo pickin' girl.
I'm goin' around this world, baby mine.

Look Up, Look Down That Lonesome Road

This is a very good example of a folksong that has been heavily influenced by the mass media. In 1929 Gene Austin and Nat Shilkret copyrighted an arrangement under the title "The Lonesome Road" that was featured in the 1929 movie version of the musical *Show Boat*. Austin (1900-1972), one of the top recording artists of the twenties, made a very successful 78 of the song that same year.

Later, well-received recordings of the piece came from Ted Lewis in 1930, Jimmie Lunceford in 1939, Tommy Dorsey in 1940 (a two-part recording), and by the Benny Goodman Quintet in 1947. Danish jazz violinist Svend Asmussen also had a popular recording of the song on a Swedish label. These, and other recordings, have made the Austin-Shilkret version a standard with jazz bands. Shilkret himself even recorded a version with a studio orchestra, and the Austin-Shilkret arrangement influenced recordings by blues musician Lonnie Johnson and gospel singer Rosetta Tharpe. In 1963 Jack Prince performed a version of the Austin-Shilkret arrangement on "The Andy Griffith Show," but by that time the song already was a pop standard.

The Austin-Shilkret version is distinguished by the lines

> *Look down, look down that lonesome road,*
> *Before you travel on.*
> *Look up, look up and greet your maker,*
> *'fore Gabriel blows his horn.*
>
> *Life is so weary and such a load,*
> *Traveling down that long, lonesome road.*

These lyrics did not originate with Austin and Shilkret, but they are rare in traditional versions collected prior to 1929. Most of these earlier versions contain verses usually associated with "In the Pines" and "There's More Pretty Girls Than One." Other frequently employed lyrics have the lines "You've slighted me once / You've slighted me twice" and conclude with "You'll never slight me any more" plus verses about "the blackest crow that ever was seen." None of these traditional lyrics are found in the 1929 pop song. It does, however, contain the image of the lonely road which is also found in all the traditional versions and also appears as an element in other songs.

The age of this song is unknown, though most estimates place it at about a hundred years, meaning that it originated around 1890. Henry Belden and Arthur Palmer Hudson suggest that the image of the lonely road is derived from black spirituals, an ascription with which several other authorities agree. This connection also brings to mind another matter about which there is great debate, namely, whether this song originated among black or white people. The vote is about equally split between those who support African-American origin and those who opt for Caucasian origin, and texts reported to date support both sides equally. In other words, for every text collected from a black singer, there is one collected from a white singer. Still, there is no argument about where the song is popular in oral tradition: it has been collected as a folksong only in the South.

The present text is from the singing of Buell Hilton Kazee, Winchester, Kentucky, and was recorded in 1972 by Mark Wilson. The two men planned to put the piece on an album intended for release later the same year, but the proposed LP was abandoned, though it did appear six years later on a posthumous record. Kazee (1900-1976) was a native of Magoffin County, Kentucky, whose parents were noted singers. His mother, Abbie Jane, was known locally as a ballad singer, while his father, John Franklin Kazee, was better known as a singer of hymns. Buell had a brief recording career from 1927 to 1929, cutting fifty-eight sides for the Brunswick label. One result of the Brunswick releases was that he was offered an opportunity to appear on the then-popular WLS National Barn Dance in Chicago. Kazee, however, did not wish that kind of life and, instead, spent over forty years earning his living as a minister in various Kentucky churches.

During the folk "revival" of the 1960s, Kazee was, like many other early country recording artists, "rediscovered" and appeared at a number of folk festivals and at college campuses during the last fifteen years of his life. His obviously trained voice (he studied music and vocal techniques at Georgetown College in Kentucky before beginning his recording career) did not meet with universal approval on the folk-festival circuit and among academic folklorists. One folksong scholar called him "the greatest white male folk singer in the United States," but another person prominent in the folk festival movement sneeringly referred to him as "boiled kazoo." While his vocal technique did not appeal to those who preferred their folksinging with a rough edge, there is no denying that his repertoire was learned in the best folk tradition.

Kazee's singing style was not the only way in which he differed from the folksinger of stereotype. He was a college-educated man who was very eloquent and, in fact, was a published author. Two of his books appeared during his lifetime, and three other volumes—a work on banjo techniques, an autobiography, and a theological tome—were in various stages of completion at the time of his death. He also composed a cantata, an operetta, and a number of songs. It was impossible to romanticize Kazee as an illiterate, Elizabethan-speaking backwoodsman, as many people are wont to do with Southern mountaineers; and that, one suspects, is the real reason some writers have such an intense dislike for his music.

Kazee's version of "Look Up, Look Down That Lonesome Road" contains several verses common to "In the Pines" and at least one stanza most often associated with "Prisoner's Song." The former is commonly encountered in this song; the latter, less so. With its eleven verses, this is easily one of the longest versions of the song recorded to date. Like most other versions, the melody has a blues feel, though it is not technically a blues number.

Look Up, Look Down that Lonesome Road

RECORDED BY MARK WILSON FROM THE SINGING OF BUELL KAZEE, WINCHESTER, KENTUCKY, 1972. MUSIC TRANSCRIPTION BY DAN BRACKIN. LYRIC TRANSCRIPTION BY W.K. McNEIL.

Look up, look down that lonesome road.
Hang down your head and cry.

True love, true love, what have I done,
That you should treat me so?

You've cause me to walk that lonesome road
That I've never walked before.

The longest train I ever saw
Was on that Georgia line.

The engine went down at six o'clock,
And the cab went down at nine.

The prettiest girl in this wide world
Was standing on behind.

The whistle blew, and the bell did ring,
The engine rolled ahead.

The train did wreck in a mile of town,
And killed my true love dead.

If I had wings like Noah's dove,
I'd fly to my true love's door.

I'd walk the porch from post to post,
Hang down my head and cry.

Look up, look down that lonesome road,
Hang down your head and cry.

Bird Song

Most folksong authorities maintain that this lyric is ultimately derived from "The Three Ravens," a Child ballad that was first printed in 1611. If so, it has been filtered through some subsequent source, most likely one associated with professional entertainment. As Vance Randolph notes, a comic, minstrel version of this piece was once popular in America, and it seems likely that the present song echoes that minstrel item. This connection is most evident in the line "what makes the white folks hate us so" that is one of the song's most stable lyrics. If "Bird Song" was originally a ballad, it has long since lost its narrative content to become mainly a catalogue of the comments by several talking birds. Of those texts that do not clearly belong to "The Three Ravens," only the variant reported by Alton Morris maintains a story and, interestingly, also has the longest text reported to date.

There is considerable variation in the birds mentioned, with a crow, hawk, blackbird, redbird, crane, woodpecker, bobwhite, hummingbird, owl, robin, turtle dove, tomtit, and sapsucker all being used. Even so, the blackbird, crow, woodpecker, redbird, and robin most often appear in versions of the song. There is also considerable variation in titles for the song—but it is often unclear whether those reported were used by the informants or merely supplied by the collectors. They include, in addition to the one used here, "The Hated Blackbird and the Crow," "The Blackbird and the Crow," "Said the Blackbird to the Crow," "The Crow Song," "Too Hoo, Says de Owl," and "Sapsuck A-Sucking Up a Hollow Gum Tree." Besides the already-mentioned verse about "white folks," the most stable lyric elements are comments on the fickleness of women and on pulling up corn.

The present text was collected in 1957 by George Foss from the singing of Marybird McAllister, Brown's Cove, Virginia. McAllister was a singer with a huge repertoire of ballads and folksongs, many of which were unusual or not otherwise widely reported. Although her specific sources of songs are not given, it is certain that they came to her from oral tradition because she was illiterate.

Bird Song

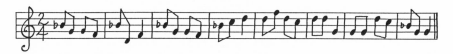

COLLECTED BY GEORGE FOSS FROM MARYBIRD MCALLISTER, BROWN'S COVE, VIRGINIA, 1957. MUSIC AND LYRIC TRANSCRIPTIONS BY GEORGE FOSS.

(O) Says the robin as he run
"Wished I had a bottle of rum
And a pretty little girl a' sittin' on my knee
Lord, how happy I would be."

Says the little humming bird,
"I would go if I wasn't so small.
I am so small I can't get a wife
'Mongst these flowers I'll spend my life."

Says the peckerwood to the crow
"What makes the white folks hate us so
Ever since ole Satan's been born
It's been our trade for to pull up corn."

Says the owl with his two shiny eyes
"This dark lonesome night
O the best of courting I've heard say
Court all night and sleep all day."

Little Sparrow

In his notes for Edna Ritchie's Folk-Legacy album, D.K. Wilgus referred to this "warning song" as one of the most beautiful found in the southern Appalachians. As the bibliographic entries given here make clear, the popularity of this piece is not confined to that region. It also has been collected from traditional singers in Florida, New York, Missouri, Arkansas, and Indiana. Still, the vast majority of versions reported to date are from southern Appalachia—though whether this reflects a greater enjoyment of the song there than in other parts of the country is debatable. It may. But it may just as well indicate nothing more than greater collecting activity in that region than in other parts of the United States.

Many authorities believe this piece is quite old, possibly more than three hundred years. This dating is based on the assumption that the lyric is derived from the Scottish ballad "Jamie Douglas," the earliest-known published version of which appeared in Allan Ramsay's *Tea-Table Miscellany* (1727). Even then, it was considered an old song. The ballad supposedly recounts the unhappy marriage between Lady Barbara Erskine and James, the second Marquis of Douglas. Married in 1670, the couple divorced in 1681—their separation caused largely, according to tradition, by the slanderous accusations of William Lawrie, the marquis's principal chamberlain, against the marchioness. The 1727 version of "Jamie Douglas," called "Waly, Waly, Gin Love Be Bony," includes the following verse that is echoed in most versions of "Little Sparrow:"

> *O waly, waly! but love be bony*
> *A little time while it is new;*
> *But when 't is auld, it waxeth cauld,*
> *And fades away like morning dew.*

The song also contains a later verse that is commonly encountered in versions of "Little Sparrow":

But had I wist, before I kissed,
  That love had been sae ill to win,
I'd lock'd my heart in a case of gold,
  And pin'd it with a silver pin.

No published eighteenth-century version, however, has verses about the sparrow, the most important and consistent image in versions of "Little Sparrow." Indeed, the use of the sparrow image apparently is fairly recent. At least, no texts with verses about the sparrow have surfaced that predate 1900, though two versions collected in the twentieth century probably were learned earlier. In *Ballads and Songs Collected by the Missouri Folk-Lore Society,* Henry M. Belden prints a text titled "Warning" that came from a C.H. Williams, Bollinger County, Missouri, in 1906. Williams said, "I was very young when I learned this and don't remember who I heard sing it first." Belden doesn't provide information about Williams's age, but it seems almost certain that he learned the song sometime before 1900. Mrs. C.S. McClellan of High Springs, Florida, included lyrics about the sparrow in her version of "Fair and Tender Ladies" that she sang for Alton Morris. Mrs. McClellan learned the song from her mother, and, though Morris fails to give details about Mrs. McClellan's age, it is entirely possible that this information dates her version prior to the twentieth century.

Until relatively recently, the bird association was often with a swallow rather than a sparrow. For example, two texts collected in 1916 by Cecil Sharp, in Carmen, North Carolina, and Flag Pond, Tennessee, use the swallow rather than the sparrow. Possibly the swallow is the older usage, employed before the twentieth century. Mrs. G.A. Griffin of Newberry, Florida, one of Alton Morris's star informants, made the association with the swallow in her version of "Come All You Fair and Pretty Ladies," a song she learned from her father many years earlier when she was a child in Georgia. Most likely, this dates her version of her song back to the late nineteenth century. Of course, it is entirely possible that a more generic term was used before either "sparrow" or "swallow" became common. This likelihood is suggested by a text reported by Henry Belden from a manuscript songbook kept by a James Ashby of Holt County, Missouri. Ashby's text, dated August 6, 1877, has the line "I wish I was a little black bird."

Although such titles as "Say Oh! Beware," "Warning," and "A Wish" have been reported by various collectors, the two titles most often used are "Little Sparrow" and "Come All You Fair and Tender Ladies." Until the last three decades, both titles were used about equally, but since about 1960 most singers have preferred "Fair and Tender Ladies" or "Come All You Fair and Tender Ladies." The greater frequency of this title possibly reflects the influence of a 1952 recording by The Carter Sisters and Mother Maybelle. On this 78 Helen, Anita, and June each take a turn singing a verse solo backed by Maybelle's autoharp playing, and the entire group joins in singing the chorus. This record (released as Columbia CO-47680) was a respectable though not huge seller, but its influence has extended far beyond initial sales.

The present text of "Little Sparrow" was collected in 1962 by George Foss from the singing of Florence Shiflett, Wyatt's Mountain, Virginia. Shiflett, born in 1876, was a member of a family well known locally as singers. A sister, Etta Ritchie, was one of the noted collector Richard Chase's major informants when he came into the region on a ballad- and folksong-collecting expedition. Other relatives contributed to Cecil Sharp's collection during the 1920s. Her cousin, Robert Shiflett, sang many songs and performed several items of non-musical lore for Foss. Florence Shiflett's text includes the sparrow association and comments about the perfidy of young men, in which they are compared to stars of a summer's morning; but the lyrics about locking up the heart—the third most stable lyric element in versions of "Little Sparrow"—are not included. There is no indication where Shiflett learned this song, but it seems likely that it came from a member of her family.

Little Sparrow

COLLECTED BY GEORGE FOSS FROM FLORENCE SHIFLETT, WYATT'S MOUNTAIN, VIRGINIA, 1962. MUSIC AND LYRIC TRANSCRIPTIONS BY GEORGE FOSS.

Come all you maids and pretty fair maidens,
Take warning how that you love young men;
They're like the bright star in a summer's morning,
First appear and then are gone.

It's once I had a own true lover,
Indeed I really thought he was my own;
Straight way he went and he courted another
And left me here to weep and moan.

I wish I was a little sparrow,
Or some of those birds that fly so high;
It's after my true love I would follow,
And when he talked I would be nigh.

When he was talking to some other,
A-telling her of many those fine things;
It's on his bosom I would flutter
With my little tender wings.

But now I ain't no little sparrow,
Nor none of those birds that fly so high;
I'll go home full of grief and sorrow
And sing and pass the time by.

My Home's Across the Smoky Mountains

This song is also known as "My Home's Across the Blue Ridge Mountains," and under that title it was recorded by the Carolina Tar Heels on April 3, 1929, for the Victor Talking Machine Company. Guitarist Clarence Ashley was credited as the composer on that recording, but it is very doubtful that the song originated with him. It was common practice in pre-World War II country recordings to copyright any song that was in public domain. It seems likely that the song was at least as old as Ashley (1895-1967) when it was recorded in 1929. This recording may have helped make the song more widely known—though perhaps recordings by the Carter Family, the Delmore Brothers, and Fiddling Arthur Smith during the 1930s were more important in increasing the song's popularity. A later version of The Carolina Tar Heels also recorded the song in 1961.

Despite, or perhaps because of, the song's frequent appearance on commercial records, it has generally been overlooked by folksong collectors. The earliest references in academic folksong books are two texts in the *Frank C. Brown Collection of North Carolina Folklore*. The first, recorded in June 1948 from the singing of Bascom Lamar Lunsford, is four verses in length. The second, an undated two-verse text from an unidentified informant, bears the title "I'm Going Over Rocky Mountain." In 1954 Leonard Roberts collected a version titled "Icy Mountain" from a Kentucky singer, Jim Couch (a pseudonym), who claimed to have heard it as a youth, i.e., in the early years of the twentieth century. This is the farthest back the song has been definitely dated, though it may well predate the twentieth century.

In 1959 Frank Warner collected the song under the title "I'm Goin' Back to North Carolina" from Frank Proffitt of Reese, North Carolina. Proffitt claimed it was a well-known banjo tune that he used to play and sing when he performed with a group at local dances and parties. Warner's opinion was that Proffitt either wrote some of the lyrics or at least rearranged them to suit his mood. The latter seems more likely since the verses are relatively simple and are all very traditional-sounding. Even so, Proffitt was a performer who well knew what folksong collectors were looking for and certainly was capable of producing a traditional-sounding lyric whenever he wanted.

The only other folksong collector to publish a version of this song is Art Rosenbaum. In 1977 he recorded "My Home's in Charlotte, North Carolina" from the singing of Lawrence Eller, Upper Hightower, Georgia. This text, to date the only one that refers to a specific town, was remembered by Eller from the singing of his mother. He recalled that when he was a small child (in the late nineteen-teens) his mother sang this song while she worked at the spinning wheel. Lawrence himself sang it either a cappella or to banjo accompaniment.

The present text is from the singing of Bascom Lamar Lunsford, who had it from Lou Greer of the Catawba River Valley in western North Carolina. It is instructive to compare this version with the one recorded from Lunsford in 1948, presumably from the same source. The present text is one verse longer (the fourth verse is not in the Brown version), and the lyric is changed from second to first person.

My Home's Across the Smoky Mountains

FROM THE SINGING OF BASCOM LAMAR LUNSFORD. MUSIC TRANSCRIPTION BY JOHN M. FORBES.
LYRIC TRANSCRIPTION BY LOYAL JONES.

My home's across the Smoky Mountains.
My home's across the Smoky Mountains.
My home's across the Smoky Mountains,
And I'll never get to see you anymore.

Goodbye my little Sugar Darlin'.
Goodbye my little Sugar Darlin'.
Goodbye my little Sugar Darlin'.
I'll never get to see you anymore.

Rock my baby, feed it candy.
Rock my baby, feed it candy.
Rock my baby, feed it candy.
'Cause I'll never get to see it anymore.

I'm leavin' on a Monday morning.
I'm leavin' on a Monday morning.
I'm leavin' on a Monday morning.
And I'll never get to see you anymore.

My home's across the Smoky Mountains.
My home's across the Smoky Mountains.
My home's across the Smoky Mountains.
And I'll never get to see you anymore.

Free Little Bird

This song is related to the "Kitty Kline" set of lyrics, distinguished by the "take me home" and the "free little bird" themes. As Vance Randolph has shown, it also bears some relationship to the song variously titled "Nobody Cares For Me" or "I Wish I Was a Little Bird" and to some versions of "On the Banks of the Old Tennessee." Henry Belden also noted its relationship to some variants of "Little Sparrow."

To complicate matters further, "Kitty Kline" is sometimes also merged with portions of "Kitty Clyde," a popular song of 1853 written by one L.V.H. Crosby. In the earliest published report of "Kitty Kline," in 1909 by Louise Rand Bascom, it is labeled "the ballad which is most universally known" in western North Carolina; Bascom even suggests that it "might be called the national song of the highlanders." Even at that time, the song existed in very diverse forms having, according to Bascom, almost "as many versions as there are singers." This situation suggests either that the original song was quite ancient and had been around long enough for numerous variants and versions to crop up or that several similar originals had merged over a relatively short time. The latter seems more likely, though one cannot be certain, especially since the pre-twentieth-century ancestry of "Kitty Kline" has not been traced.

One of the interesting suggestions made by Bascom is that the song "Kitty Kline" is peculiar to the Tennessee-North Carolina mountain region. That is incorrect, as the second text in the present collection shows. This version, by Bob Blair, Mountain View, Arkansas, does not mention "Kitty Kline;" but then, neither does the first of two versions given by Bascom. That Bascom text does, however, include verses beginning "Oh, I can't stay hyar by myself," "If I was a little fish," and "If I was a sparrer bird," all of which are quite similar to Blair's song.

Even more interesting is Bascom's reference to the song as a ballad. If it ever was a ballad, it has long since lost its narrative: no reported version, including those in Bascom's article, contains anything like a connected story. This fact may indicate that Bascom uses the word "ballad" in a loose, and ultimately meaningless, way. On the other hand, one should not be too quick to toss out the possibility that "Kitty Kline" was originally a ballad which, once its story began to disappear, started picking up lines, recombining them, dropping them, and taking up others, until as Henry Belden and Arthur Palmer Hudson note in their discussion of "Kitty Kline" in volume 3 of *The Frank C. Brown Collection of North Carolina Folklore*, "it is hardly possible to say whether a given text is to be reckoned a form of a particular song or not."

Although versions and variants of "Kitty Kline" still are popular in the southern Appalachian region, it is doubtful that the piece still qualifies as the most popular traditional song even in western North Carolina. It would be going too far to say that the song owes its current vogue to commercial or mass media sources, but it is undeniable that fairly frequent recording by country musicians has not harmed its traditional status. It seems to have had particular appeal to artists from Georgia and Tennessee, for most of the early recordings were by performers from those two states. Apparently, the first commercial recording was by banjoist Land Norris, whose version on the Okeh label was titled "Little Birdie." Subsequently, Dykes' Magic City Trio and the Roane County Ramblers, both from Tennessee, and Clayton McMichen, originally from Georgia, were among the several artists who recorded the song. In fact, McMichen recorded it twice, as "Free Little Bird Number 1" and "Free Little Bird Number 2."

One of the more interesting commercially issued versions—and possibly the best selling—was recorded in October 1928 by yet another Tennessee group, the Allen Brothers. Austin (1901-1959) and Lee Allen (1906-1984) were natives of Franklin County, Tennessee, and one of the most popular country duets of the late 1920s and early 1930s. Stylistically they leaned towards the blues, and some bluesiness is evident in their version, which is taken at a slower pace than most country recordings of the song. Two guitars, a banjo and a fiddle back up the vocal on their version, and the tune utilized is strongly reminiscent of "Kitty Clyde" and "On the Banks of the Old Tennessee." Their lyrics, which are given below, include several of the lines common to other versions but contain a closing verse that is rarely encountered:

> *Just a free little bird as I can be,*
> *Just a free little bird as I can be,*
> *For I'm sitting on a hillside, weeping all the day*
> *No sweetheart to grieve after me.*
>
> *Oh, bring me a chair and I'll sit down,*
> *Just a pen and ink I'll write it down,*
> *And every line that I write down*
> *I guess I'm going to the ground.*
>
> *Oh if I were a little bird*
> *I would never build on the ground.*
> *But I'd build my nest on my true lover's breast*
> *Where the bad boys could not tear it down.*
>
> *Oh if I were a little fish*
> *I would never swim in the sea.*
> *But I'd swim in the brook, where poor Katy hung her hook*
> *On the banks of the old Tennessee.*
>
> *It is sweet to be drinking of ale,*
> *It is sweet to be drinking of wine,*
> *But the sweetest is to sit by that darling girl's side*
> *That stole away this tender heart of mine.*

The first version given here is from the singing of Bascom Lamar Lunsford, who collected it from Tom Boyd, Buncombe County, North Carolina. Like many versions of "Free Little Bird," it contains verses usually associated with "The Lass of Roch Royal" (Child 76), which is common in many versions of "Kitty Kline." Then come the characteristic "free little bird" and "take me home" verses, followed by two less common verses—the fifth being essentially the same as the last verse of the Allen Brothers' recording of "Free Little Bird."

As already noted, "I Can't Stay Here By Myself" is from the singing of Bob Blair, collected in 1979 by W.K. McNeil. Blair (1932-1989) was a storehouse of traditional balladry and folksong, much of which he learned from his family. He apparently acquired this lyric number from his father. This is the longest reported text to date of this form of "Free Little Bird." It lacks the "I wisht I was a little boy" and "But as I am a little girl" verses found in the 1909 text from West Plains, Missouri, given by Henry Belden in *Ballads and Songs Collected by the Missouri Folklore Society* (1940).

Free Little Bird

FROM THE SINGING OF BASCOM LAMAR MUNSFORD. MUSIC TRANSCRIPTION BY JOHN M. FORBES.
LYRIC TRANSCRIPTION BY LOYAL JONES.

I'm as free a little bird as I can be.
Just as free a little bird as I can be.
I'll build my nest in the sour apple tree,
Where the bad boys will never bother me.

Oh, who will shoe them little feet,
And who will glove them little hands?
Who will kiss them red rosy cheeks
When I'm in some far distant land?

My Papa will shoe these little feet,
And my Mama will glove these little hands,
But you may kiss these red rosy cheeks,
When we're in some far distant land.

Take me home, little birdie, take me home.
Take me home by the light of the moon.
While the moon is shining bright and the stars are getting light,
Take me home to my Mama, take me home.

Oh, it's very good drinking of the ale,
And it's very good drinking of the wine.
But it's better by far, sittin' by that blue-eyed boy
That's stole this tender heart of mine.

Oh, the willow tree may fade,
And the willow tree may twine,
But I never will prove false to the one I love best,
That's stole away this tender heart of mine.

I Can't Stay Here by Myself

COLLECTED BY W.K. McNEIL FROM BOB BLAIR, PLEASANT GROVE, ARKANSAS, 1979. MUSIC AND LYRIC
TRANSCRIPTIONS BY W.K. McNEIL.

Oh I wish I was a little bird,
I'd fly through the top of a tree,
I'd fly and sing a sad little song,
I can't stay here by myself.

I can't stay here by myself,
I can't stay here by myself.
I'd fly and sing a sad little song,
I can't stay here by myself.

Once I had plenty money,
My friends all around me would stand.
Now my pockets are empty
And I have not a friend in the land.

Farewell, farewell corn whiskey,
Farewell peach brandy too.
You've robbed my pockets of silver
And I have no use for you.

Oh, I wish I was a little fish,
I'd swim to the bottom of the sea.
I'd swim and sing a sad little song,
I can't stay here by myself.

I Wish I Was a Mole in the Ground

This lyric number was one of the favorite songs of Bascom Lamar Lunsford, and it is his version that is presented here. Lunsford learned the song about 1901 from Fred Moody, Jonathan's Creek, North Carolina, a classmate at Rutherford College. All but one of the printed versions published to date come either from Lunsford or Moody. The latter also sang the song in 1921 for Frank C. Brown or the person who contributed the song to Brown's collection. Yet the song is more widely known in tradition than existing publications indicate. Art Rosenbaum's text, from Chesley Chancey of Cherry Log, Gilmer County, Georgia, is proof that the song is known outside western North Carolina. In a 1929 publication, *30 and 1 Folk Songs*, Lunsford offered the opinion that the song was a "typical product of the Pigeon River Valley." Henry Belden and Arthur Palmer Hudson, editors of the ballad and folksong sections of *The Frank C. Brown Collection of North Carolina Folklore*, suggested that the song probably originated either on the minstrel stage or among roustabouts. Any of these three origins is quite possible, but none has been proven yet.

It is instructive to compare Lunsford's 1929 printing with the present text. In the earlier version, the verse about Tempe is omitted and the question-and-answer format is missing. The most likely explanation for these differences is that Lunsford either intentionally or unintentionally changed the lyrics over the years, but it is possible that the changes were dictated for some reason by the publisher of the 1929 collection. Even that 1929 version differs from Moody's original, assuming that it was identical to the text contained in the Brown collection (admittedly a risky assumption). The version Moody supplied Brown is longer than any of those published or recorded by Lunsford: it includes a sixth verse beginning "Oh, Tempy, let your hair roll down" that, as Belden and Hudson note, is derived from "Alberta." The version collected by Rosenbaum is shorter than Lunsford's, omitting all but the first and last verse given here, but the lyrics are not given in the same order. Lunsford's fifth verse is the second one in the Rosenbaum text, and the Georgia version concludes with the first verse being repeated. A verse beginning "I'll take you to your mamma next payday" not found in the other published texts is the third verse. Finally, the Georgia version differs from Lunsford's in that it is sung in two-part harmony. The several differences between the published versions reveal little more than that the song has been in oral circulation for some time.

I Wish I Was a Mole in the Ground

FROM THE SINGING OF BASCOM LAMAR LUNSFORD. MUSIC TRANSCRIPTION BY JOHN M. FORBES. LYRIC TRANSCRIPTION BY LOYAL JONES.

> I wish I was a mole in the ground.
> Yes I wish I was a mole in the ground.
> If I's a mole in the ground I'd root that mountain down,
> And I wish I was a mole in the ground.
>
> Oh, Tempe wants a nine-dollar shawl.
> Yes, Tempe wants a nine-dollar shawl.
> When I come o'er the hill with a forty-dollar bill,
> Tis, baby where you been so long?
>
> Oh, where have you been so long?
> Yes, where have you been so long?
> I've been in the Bend with the rough and rowdy men,
> It's baby where you been so long?

Oh, I don't like a railroad man,
No, I don't like a railroad man.
A railroad man will kill you when he can,
And he'll drink up your blood like wine.

I wish I was a lizard in the spring.
Yes, I wish I was a lizard in the spring.
If I's a lizard in the spring I could hear my darlin' sing,
I wish I was a lizard in the spring.

Beware, Oh, Beware

This is one of those songs that might be categorized as a ballad by some authorities and as a folksong by others. It is included in the latter category here because it doesn't provide a narrative, merely descriptive verses. Vance Randolph noted its relationship to a song titled "Beware," published by Ferdinand Trifet in the March 1892 issue of *Trifet's Monthly Budget of Music*. It is, however, probably derived from a German song published in the late 1860s. While the lyrics in Trifet deal with the duplicity of women, most texts reported from traditional singers warn women against men. The song is sparsely represented in folksong collections, but it may be more popular than the published record indicates. It also is poorly represented on commercial recordings, the only non-revival performance to date being that by the West Virginia singer Blind Alfred Reed (1880-1956). His version, titled "Beware," was recorded in New York City on December 3, 1929, for the Victor label. For purposes of comparison his lyrics follow:

> *We know young men are bold and free,*
> *Beware, oh take care,*
> *They tell you they're friends but they're liars you see,*
> *Beware, oh take care.*

> CHORUS:
> *Beware young ladies, they're fooling you,*
> *Trust them not, they're fooling you,*
> *Beware young ladies, they're fooling you,*
> *Beware, oh take care.*

> *They smoke, they chew, they wear fine shoes,*
> *Beware, oh take care,*
> *And in their pocket is a bottle of booze,*
> *Beware, oh take care.*

> CHORUS *(same as before)*

Around their neck they wear a guard,
Beware, oh take care,
And in their pocket is a deck of cards,
Beware, oh take care.

CHORUS *(same as before)*

They put their hands up to their hearts,
They sigh, oh they sigh,
They say they love no one but you,
They lie, oh they lie.

CHORUS *(same as before)*

The present text was collected March 9, 1951, by Irene Jones Carlisle from Frances Oxford, Spring Valley, Arkansas. Mrs. Oxford had lived near Spring Valley all her life, and her songs were learned mainly from members of her family and from friends in her childhood. Carlisle offered this description of the woman: "Mrs. Oxford is robust and vivacious; she sings in a shrill and breathless voice, but she enjoys singing, and has a very fine memory for the words of the songs." When she was about twelve years old, Mrs. Oxford learned her version of "Beware, Oh, Beware" from Hap Bragg, a resident of Spring Valley.

Beware, Oh, Beware

COLLECTED BY IRENE JONES CARLISLE FROM FRANCES OXFORD, SPRING VALLEY, ARKANSAS, MARCH 9, 1951. MUSIC TRANSCRIPTION BY MRS. HOWARD R. CLARK. LYRIC TRANSCRIPTION BY IRENE JONES CARLISLE.

There are young men both bold and free;
Beware, oh, beware;
They can both false and friendly be;
Take care, oh, take care.

Take care, young girls, they're fooling you;
Beware, oh beware;
I'll tell you what, they'll lie to you;
Take care, oh, take care.

His hair is of a chestnut hue;
Beware, oh, beware,
He combs and he curls, and it's just for you;
Take care, oh, take care.

Around his neck he wears a garb,
Beware, oh, beware,
And in his pocket a deck of cards;
Take care, oh, take care.

He can't support a good mustache,
Beware, oh, beware,
And around the girls he cuts a dash;
Take care, oh, take care.

He puts his hand upon his heart;
He sighs, oh, he sighs;
He says he's pierced with a Cupid's dart,
But he lies, oh, he lies.

He smokes and he chews and he thinks hisself a man;
Beware, oh, beware;
And once in awhile he'll take a dram;
Take care, oh, take care.

Darling Corie

This song, a favorite of folk revival singers during the 1950s and 1960s, is usually known by the title given here—though, as folklorist Leonard Roberts noted in his book *Sang Branch Settlers*, it has a variety of other, less commonly used titles. A version collected by Cecil Sharp in Burnsville, North Carolina, in 1918 has the title "The Gambling Man," but is unclear whether that title came from Sharp's informant, Mrs. Clercy Deeton, or from Sharp himself. The same is true of "Hustling Gamblers," collected by Josiah H. Combs in 1913 in Hindman, Kentucky; and this confusion also exists for other reported titles.

The most consistent elements in this lyric song are the command for the girl to wake up and the comments about the first or last time the narrator has seen her. Many versions also contain the lines about digging a hole in the meadow or ground. Although most versions emphasize the protagonist's waking, the following verse Sharp collected from Mrs. Deeton does not: "Last night as I lay on my pillow / Last night as I lay on my bed / Last night as I lay on my pillow / I dreamed little Bessy was dead."

Probably the first commercial recording of "Darling Corey" was by Buell Hilton Kazee, who cut a version in New York City, April 20, 1927, for the Brunswick label. Kazee (1900-1976) recorded prolifically during the years 1927-1929. Like many other early country artists, he was "discovered" by the folk revival audience of the 1950s and 1960s; two albums of his work were released, one in 1958 and the other posthumously in 1978. Kazee's style of singing, however, was not typical of Southern mountain folksingers. Instead, he sounded very much like a trained singer, which he was (he took vocal classes at Georgetown College in Kentucky and later was a voice instructor). But many of his songs came from a genuine folk tradition.

B.F. Shelton (1902-1963), a Corbin, Kentucky barber, recorded the song in Bristol, Tennessee, July 29, 1927 for the Victor Talking

Machine Company. Like Kazee's, Shelton's version (probably the second commercially recorded rendition of the song) featured a banjo-accompanied vocal. But his singing was closer to the conventional traditional sound than Kazee's.

The present version of "Darling Corie" is from the singing of Bradley Kincaid. He learned the song from his brother-in-law, Dr. John Baker, who was a native of Manchester, Kentucky, but who spent most of his adult life in the college town of Berea, Kentucky. The "highway robbers" mentioned here are, in most reported versions, "revenue officers" or just "revenuers." Although Kincaid made numerous commercial recordings in 1927-1928, he never put this song on 78 or LP.

Darling Corie

FROM THE SINGING OF BRADLEY KINCAID. MUSIC TRANSCRIPTION BY JOHN M. FORBES. LYRIC TRANSCRIPTION BY LOYAL JONES.

Wake up, wake up, Darling Corie,
And go get me my gun;
The highway robbers are a-coming,
And I'll die before I run.

Dig a hole in the meadow,
Dig a hole in the ground,
Dig a hole in the meadow
And lay Darling Corie down.

Wake up, wake up, Darling Corie,
What makes you sleep so sound?
The highway robbers are coming
And they'll tear your playhouse down.

Last time I saw Darling Corie
Was on the banks of deep blue sea,
Two pistols around her body
And a banjo on her knee.

Wake up, wake up, Darling Corie,
And go get me my gun;
I ain't no man for trouble,
But trouble has just begun.

Dig a hole in the meadow,
Dig a hole in the ground,
Dig a hole in the meadow
And lay Darling Corie down.

Little Turtle Dove

For at least three hundred years the turtle dove has appeared in various lyric songs dealing with love. This is because the bird is characterized by its devotion to its mate, and thus makes a perfect symbol of enduring love. Songs containing lines about the turtle dove are called "The True Lover's Farewell," "False Hearted Lover," "Little Dove," "Lonesome Dove" and "The Storms Are On the Ocean," in addition to the title given here. Frequently these lyrics combine elements from "The Lass of Roch Royal" and the motif of going up on a mountain, as found in "Old Smoky," "Cindy," and several other traditional songs. The most stable element in the various forms of "Little Turtle Dove," however, is the first verse given in the present text, found in almost every variant reported to date. The lines about marrying, or not marrying, in various seasons of the year also crop up on a regular basis. The verse "The hog is in the pen" appears in various songs and also is the lead verse of a piece titled "Hog (or Pig) in the Pen" that is particularly popular with amateur bluegrass musicians.

According to George Pullen Jackson, a song titled "Lonesome Grove," by William C. Davis, that appeared in the religious songbook *The Social Harp* (1855) was inspired by the first line of the present song. It seems that some singers have incorporated the Davis song, or parts of it, into the "turtle dove" song given here, as is demonstrated by the version reported by Leonard Roberts in *In the Pine*. When the Carter Family recorded the song as "The Storms Are On the Ocean," the dove became plural and also "mournful." This recording, which was quite popular, has certainly influenced traditional versions.

The present text is from the singing of Bascom Lamar Lunsford, who learned it in 1901 from Letch Reynolds, Buncombe County, North Carolina. Reynolds, a fellow student at Rutherford College with Lunsford, later sang the song for Frank C. Brown or one of the collectors who contributed to Brown's collection. The two versions differ mainly in the way verses are ordered. The Brown text, however, also has two verses beginning "I went up on the mountain." In 1929, in *30 and 1 Folk Songs*, Lunsford published a version of "Little Turtle Dove" that differs from that printed here mainly in the omission of the third verse. In that publication, Lunsford asserts that the first verse is derived from early English folk balladry, while the others "were added during the pioneer days of this mountain section." No documentation is offered for this viewpoint—one with which most folksong specialists would disagree.

Little Turtle Dove

FROM THE SINGING OF BASCOM LAMAR LUNSFORD. MUSIC TRANSCRIPTION BY JOHN M. FORBES. LYRIC TRANSCRIPTION BY LOYAL JONES.

Poor little turtle dove,
Sittin' in the pine.
Mournin' for its own true love,
And why not me for mine, mine,
And why not me for mine.

I'm not gonna marry in the fall.
I'll marry in the spring.
I'm gonna marry a pretty little girl,
Who wears a silver ring, ring,
Who wears a silver ring.

I'm not gonna marry in the spring of the year.
I'll marry in the fall.
I'm gonna marry a pretty little girl,
Who wears a dollar shawl, shawl,
Who wears a dollar shawl.

The hog is in the pen
And corn to feed him on.
All I want is a pretty little girl
To feed him when I'm gone, gone,
To feed him when I'm gone.

I went upon the mountain
To give my horn a blow.
And every girl in the county said,
"Yonder comes my beau, beau,
Yonder comes my beau."

The Cuckoo is a Pretty Bird

This song has a variety of titles, of which the most common is simply "The Cuckoo." Several singers also use the longer name given here. The songs "The Unconstant Lover," "Old Smokey," and "The Waggoner's Lad" are thought to derive from "The Cuckoo." This parent number has yet to be definitively traced, but it dates at least from the eighteenth century and is probably considerably older. According to Vance Randolph, a stanza about the cuckoo and its glad tidings appears in a song given in David Herd's *Ancient and Modern Scottish Songs* (1776). A nursery form of the song can be dated 1796, while another form of the lyric song was published in Glasgow in 1802. Of course, the single verse about the cuckoo and its glad tidings appears in a number of songs, such as that printed in Belden's Missouri collection (p. 476). That verse is the one constant in versions of this song.

The cuckoo is a lowly regarded bird that is used symbolically in many ways in western Europe. Because it lays its eggs in the nests of other birds, it often stands for adultery. It also is considered a harbinger of summer in Britain, and perhaps both this seasonal and a sexual sense are evident in most versions. Clearly, the latter is more prominent in the text given here. This version is from the singing of Bradley Kincaid, who learned it from his father. Kincaid was one of many commercial country artists who recorded the song, his version being cut July 12, 1928, in Chicago for the Starr Piano Company and later released on the Gennett label. The first two verses are uncommon and possibly derive from the British broadside ballad sometimes known as "Green Beds." Also uncommon are the last two lines of the fifth verse, which seem to be borrowed from "Rye Whisky." Verses four, six, and seven are usually associated with "Old Smoky," while verses three and nine are generally part of "The Unconstant Lover."

The Cuckoo is a Pretty Bird

FROM THE SINGING OF BRADLEY KINCAID. MUSIC TRANSCRIPTION BY JOHN M. FORBES. LYRIC
TRANSCRIPTION BY LOYAL JONES.

Oh, Johnny is on the water,
Let him sink or let him swim.
For if he can live without me,
I can live without him.

Johnny is a young boy,
But still younger am I;
But how often has he told me
He'd wed me or die.

O meeting is a pleasure
And parting is grief,
But an unconstant true love
Is worse than a thief.

A thief can but rob you
And take all you have,
But an unconstant lover
Will take you to your grave.

I'll take off this black dress
And I'll flourish in green,
For I don't care if I'm forsaken
I am only nineteen.
Hiccough, O Lordy, how bad I do feel,
Hiccough, O Lordy, how bad I do feel.

The grave it will rot you
And turn you to dust;
There ain't one out of twenty
That a young girl can trust.

They will court and kiss you
And get your heart warm,
But as soon as your back's turned
They'll laugh you to scorn.

The cuckoo is a pretty bird,
She sings as she flies;
She brings us good tidings
And tells us no lies.

Forsaken, forsaken,
Forsaken am I.
He is certainly mistaken
If he thinks that I'll cry.

Time Draws Near

In the exact form given here, this song has not been reported elsewhere. Actually, it is a variant of "The False True-Lover," a song found infrequently by folksong collectors. The shoe-glove-kiss dialogue is generally thought to be derived from the ballad "The Lass of Roch Royal," but it also is a common feature of many other songs, one of them being "The False True-Lover." Indeed, this dialogue is one of the song's most typical lyrics; and its other most stable lyric elements are verses three, four, and ten here. The dialogue from "The Lass of Roch Royal" may indicate that the song dates back to the eighteenth century, when the earliest known forms of that ballad appeared. Possibly, the song is even older since it is certain that "The Lass of Roch Royal" was originally a variant of a story known in Chaucer's time. But without additional evidence it is at best risky and at worst foolhardy to date this—or any other set of lyrics—on the basis of such slim data.

The present text is from the singing of Dan Tate, Fancy Gap, Virginia, and was collected by George Foss in 1962. Tate was born in 1900 in Carroll County, Virginia, and has spent his entire life there. He became well known not only for his large stock of ballads and folksongs, but also for his banjo playing. In fact, unlike many traditional singers who perform unaccompanied, Tate usually sings the ballads and folksongs he knows to banjo accompaniment. His huge repertoire combined with his instrumental abilities made him a favorite informant for collectors of folk music as well as ballad and folksong collectors. Tate's source for the present song is not given.

Time Draws Near

COLLECTED BY GEORGE FOSS FROM DAN TATE, FANCY GAP, VIRGINIA, 1962. MUSIC AND LYRIC
TRANSCRIPTIONS BY GEORGE FOSS.

Oh, time draws near my dearest dear,
When you and I must part,
How little did you know of the grief and the woe,
That lays on my poor broken heart.

Everyday it seems like two,
And every hour like ten,
You caused me to weep when I might 'a been asleep,
And say you had lost a friend.

So I went a roving one cold winter night,
While drinking on sweet wine,
When I fell in love with this pretty little miss,
She stole this heart of mine.

For she looked like some pink colored rose,
Which blossomed in the month of June,
Or some other musical instrument,
Just newly put in tune.

So I would to the Lord that I'd never been born,
Or died when I was young,
So I never could have kissed your sweet ruby lips,
Nor heard your lying tongue.

So I'll put my foot in the bottom of the ship,
I'll sail it on the sea,
I would not have treated you, my love,
Like you have treated me.

"Now who will shoe your pretty little feet,
And who will glove your hand,
And who will kiss your sweet ruby lips,
When returned from a far off land?"

"Oh Papa will shoe my pretty little feet,
And Mama will glove my hand,
And you can kiss my sweet ruby lips,
When returned from a far off land."

And the blackest crow that ever flew,
I surely will turn white,
Whenever I prove false to you,
Bright day shall turn to night.

And the time'll roll on when the sea shall run dry,
And the rocks melt down with the sun,
I never will prove false to you,
Till all this work is done.

Religious Songs ·

I'm Workin' on a Building

This song is usually discussed as an African-American song, and it may well have originated among blacks. But, if so, it is equally certain that it is not found just among black American singers. For at least the past sixty years, it also has been performed frequently by white traditional singers—far more commonly than the sparse reports by folksong collectors indicate. This popularity with white singers may well trace from a May 8, 1934, recording by The Carter Family that was initially released on the Bluebird label. Since A.P. Carter was known for collecting folk material for recording purposes, the song may already have been in white tradition, with The Carter Family's recording simply broadening its popularity. Or the Carters may have acquired the song from African-American sources, as they were sometimes known to do. In any event, their 1934 recording proved influential in more ways that just sales figures. Most likely it was the avenue by which the song entered bluegrass repertoires and has become a standard in that subgenre of commercial country music.

Possibly this song originated as a ring shout, a type of spiritual characterized by simple lyrics that were easy to remember and also provided almost endless possibilities for expansion. Over sixty years ago, Howard W. Odum and Guy B. Johnson wrote in *The Negro and His Songs* that this song "appeals to the average Negro." The implication of that statement is that the song was very popular. Its popularity may have waned somewhat among black audiences since the 1920s, but it still is a favorite, as indicated by recent recordings by Dr. C.J. Johnson and Albertina Walker.

The present version of "I'm Workin' On a Building" was recorded in August 1973 by Dianne M. Dugaw from the singing of Jasper David Ward and Nona Hightower Ward, Canaan Mountain, Arkansas. Nona accompanied this song on guitar, but she also played piano on other songs the Wards sang for Dugaw. At the time of the recording, Nona was sixty-seven and her husband, David, seventy-two. Nona had a large repertoire of religious songs, many of which were printed in paperback gospel hymnals sold in rural areas throughout the South. Some of the other numbers she knew were recorded by early country music performers. Mrs. Ward did not necessarily obtain her texts from such mass distributed sources, but her gospel songs undoubtedly were either directly or indirectly influenced by such commercial activity. Formerly she knew and performed several secular songs, but after she was "saved" she sang only songs "of the Lord."

I'm Workin' on a Buildin'

COLLECTED BY DIANNE M. DUGAW FROM JASPER DAVID WARD AND NONA HIGHTOWER WARD, CANAAN MOUNTAIN, ARKANSAS. MUSIC AND LYRIC TRANSCRIPTIONS BY DIANNE M. DUGAW.

I'm workin' on a buildin',
I'm workin' on a buildin',
I'm workin' on a buildin',
For my Lord,
For my Lord.

If I was a singer,
Tell you what I would do,
I would just keep singin',
Workin' on a buildin' too.

I'm workin' on a buildin',
I'm workin' on a buildin',
I'm workin' on a buildin',
For my Lord,
For my Lord.

There's a Holy Ghost buildin',
There's a Holy Ghost buildin',
There's a Holy Ghost buildin',
For my Lord,
For my Lord.

If I was a preacher,
Tell you what I would do,
I'd just keep on preachin',
Workin' on a buildin' too.

I'm workin' on a buildin',
I'm workin' on a buildin',
I'm workin' on a buildin',
For my Lord,
For my Lord.

There's a Holy Ghost buildin',
There's a Holy Ghost buildin',
There's a Holy Ghost buildin',
For my Lord,
For my Lord.

Go Wash in That Beautiful Pool

This song is generally thought to refer to the story related in the Bible in II Kings 5. That entire chapter is devoted to an account of Elisha curing the Syrian captain Naaman of leprosy. One version of the song, collected in 1938 in Alliance, North Carolina, mentions Naaman but most texts omit this rather unusual name. In fact, only versions using the alternate title "Go Wash in the Beautiful Stream" feature the name; and, to date, it has been reported by folksong collectors only from the east coast of North Carolina. There is, however, a recording of this form on the Paramount label by a Reverend Moses Mason, whose biography is unknown.

"Go Wash in That Beautiful Pool" is typical of camp-meeting songs that are designed so they can be learned quickly by a large number of people. The tunes are relatively simple, with much repetition in the melodies and in the texts. Frequently they use incremental repetition—a verse being essentially the same as that preceding it, with one slight but significant change. In the present text, the only difference between verses is that new family members are introduced; indeed, the very use of relatives is a common feature of the camp-meeting song. Not that performing these songs is an easy task that can be done by everyone. To properly appreciate their power, one must hear them delivered by skilled traditional performers—artists who know the words and believe them.

Although "Go Wash in That Beautiful Pool" is one of the best known of the old camp-meeting songs, it has rarely appeared on commercial recordings. Other than Reverend Mason's already-mentioned release, the only ones are both by the late Doctor Coble Walsh, who recorded as Dock Walsh with a group known as the Carolina Tar Heels. Walsh (1901-1967) (his real first name was Doctor), from Lewis Fork, North Carolina, first recorded the song as "Bathe in That Beautiful Pool" on the Victor label in 1929. He accompanied himself using his "Hawaiian" or "knife banjo" technique, one of the few recorded instances of this style from white tradition. In 1962 Walsh recorded the song again as "Go Wash in That Beautiful Pool" on the Folk-Legacy label, this time using a straight banjo technique. In a sense, both of these recordings are non-representative because most often at camp-meetings the song was performed without instrumental accompaniment.

The present text was collected in May 1979 by W.K. McNeil from the singing of Bill and Dessie Zinn, Fifty-Six, Arkansas. During two separate sessions of about two hours each, I recorded approximately forty different songs from the Zinns, all of the pieces being old camp-meeting numbers. Both grew up during the second decade of the twentieth century and learned the items they knew at church meetings in their neighborhood.

Go Wash in That Beautiful Pool

COLLECTED BY W.K. McNEIL FROM BILL AND DESSIE ZINN, FIFTY SIX, ARKANSAS, MAY, 1979. MUSIC AND LYRIC TRANSCRIPTIONS BY W.K. McNEIL.

> My father's crossed over the river,
> He's now in the kingdom of God,
> He's now in the kingdom with the angels all 'round,
> Go wash in that beautiful pool.
>
> Go wash in that beautiful pool,
> Go wash in that beautiful pool,
> The river of life is flowing for all,
> Go wash in that beautiful pool.

My mother's crossed over the river,
She's now in the kingdom of God,
She's now in the kingdom with the angels all 'round,
Go wash in that beautiful pool.

Go wash in that beautiful pool,
Go wash in that beautiful pool,
The river of life is flowing for all,
Go wash in that beautiful pool.

My brother's crossed over the river,
He's now in the kingdom of God,
He's now in the kingdom with the angels all 'round,
Go wash in that beautiful pool.

Go wash in that beautiful pool,
Go wash in that beautiful pool,
The river of life is flowing for all,
Go wash in that beautiful pool.

My sister's crossed over the river,
She's now in the kingdom of God,
She's now in the kingdom with the angels all 'round,
Go wash in that beautiful pool.

Go wash in that beautiful pool,
Go wash in that beautiful pool,
The river of life is flowing for all,
Go wash in that beautiful pool.

My children 've crossed over the river,
They're now in the kingdom of God,
They're now in the kingdom with the angels all 'round,
Go wash in that beautiful pool.

Go wash in that beautiful pool,
Go wash in that beautiful pool,
The river of life is flowing for all,
Go wash in that beautiful pool.

Twilight Is Stealing

This song was called "Twilight Is Falling" by its author, Aldine Sillman Kieffer, when it was published in 1877. Kieffer's lyrics were set to a tune by Benjamin C. Unseld, Kieffer's associate and principal of the South's first normal school for rural singing teachers—the Virginia Normal Music School established at New Market, Virginia, in 1874. Kieffer (1840-1904) founded the *Musical Million*, a monthly musical periodical devoted to rural music, and became such a staunch apostle of shape-notes that he was called the "Don Quixote of shape-notes" by those who ridiculed the system. Of Kieffer's several songs, the ones best remembered today are "Grave on the Green Hillside," "My Mountain Home," and "Twilight Is Falling."

The present text was collected in March 1983 by W.K. McNeil from the singing of Almeda Riddle, Greers Ferry, Arkansas. Riddle (1898-1986) was long known as one of America's best and most important ballad singers. In recognition of this, she was selected in 1983 as one of the recipients of the National Endowment for the Arts Heritage Award, the first Arkansan to receive the honor. Riddle's ballad singing is well documented on a number of albums, most of which are, unfortunately, now out of print. On the other hand, her religious song tradition—always at least as important to Almeda as her ballads—is relatively poorly documented. Even *A Singer and Her Songs* (1970), the book about her life edited by Roger D. Abrahams, is primarily concerned with the secular songs, though a new edition being prepared by Abrahams and Debora Kodish may change the emphasis. Only one of Riddle's several albums, *How Firm a Foundation*, is exclusively devoted to her religious songs, and it is the last record she made.

Most of Riddle's religious songs came from the shape-note singing tradition—a majority of them, like "Twilight Is Stealing," learned from her father, J.L. James, a singing-school teacher. Although James could sing by note (as opposed to shape), he loved the shape-note songs and imparted his love of singing to his daughter.

Twilight Is Stealing

COLLECTED BY W.K. McNEIL FROM ALMEDA RIDDLE, GREERS FERRY, ARKANSAS, MARCH, 1983. MUSIC
AND LYRIC TRANSCRIPTIONS BY W.K. McNEIL.

Twilight is stealing over the lea,
Shadows are falling dark on the lea;
Borne on the nightwind, voices of yore,
Come from the far-off shore.

Far away beyond the starlit sky,
Where his lovelight never, never dies;
Gleameth a mansion filled with delight,
Sweet, happy home so bright.

Voices of loved ones, songs of my past,
They linger round me while life shall last;
Lonely I wander, sadly I roam,
Seeking that far-off home.

Far away beyond the starlit sky,
Where the lovelight never, never dies;
Gleameth a mansion filled with delight,
Sweet, happy home so bright.

Come in the twilight, come, come to me,
Bringing your message from over the sea;
Cheering my pathway, while here I roam,
Seeking my far-off home.

Far away beyond the starlight sky,
Where the lovelight never, never dies;
Gleameth a mansion filled with delight,
Sweet, happy home so bright.

I Will Arise

This unusual piece appears to be a blending of two songs, "Come, Thou Fount of Every Blessing" and "I Will Arise." A portion of the present text appears in the *Original Sacred Harp*, Denson Revision, under the title "Restoration." But only the first verse, chorus, and melody are used here; and most of the verses are from "Come, Thou Fount of Every Blessing," a hymn written in 1758 by Robert Robinson (1735-1790) and first published in *A Collection of Hymns used by the Church of Christ in Angel Alley, Bishopgate* (1759). There has been some speculation that the lyrics are the work of the countess of Huntingdon, but it is generally accepted that Robinson is the author. A native of Swaffham, England, Robinson was apprenticed in 1749 as a barber. In 1752 he heard the famous evangelist George Whitefield preach a sermon based on Matthew 3:7.

So impressed was Robinson that he became a convert to Christianity and, in 1755, began to preach. At first he pastored a Methodist church in Mindenhall, England, but shortly thereafter changed to an Independent congregation in Norwich, England. Then, in 1761, he switched denominational affiliation for the third and last time when he became pastor of the Stone Yard Baptist Church in Cambridge, a position he held until shortly before his death in 1790. A man with no formal education, Robinson nevertheless became well known as a preacher, scholar, and theologian. He wrote many theological works, but this was his only hymn to achieve any widespread popularity. It first appeared in the United States in *The Christian Duty, Exhibited in a Series of Hymns Collected From Various Authors* (1791). Robinson's lyrics, but not his tune, have been extremely popular with folk singers.

A poem titled "I Will Arise," from which the chorus used here is taken, was published by a Joseph Hart in 1759 and set, by some unknown person, to a tune thought to be of camp-meeting origin. Hart (1712-1768) became a religious convert in 1757 after hearing

John Wesley preach. He himself immediately began preaching and continued to do so until his death. Under the title "Beach Spring," a version of Hart's text appears in the *Original Sacred Harp*, Denson Revision, but both the melody and words differ from the version given here. A third version appears in George P. Jackson's *Spiritual Folk Songs of Early America*, the chorus and melody of which are very similar to the present version.

The text presented here is from the singing of the Williams Family, Roland, Arkansas, a group consisting of Bob and Bonnie Williams and their five children, Autumn, Tina, Heather, Wade, and Nick. Both Bob and Bonnie come from musical families, but most of the ballads and folksongs they know seem to have come from Bonnie's family. Her parents, John Wesley Mann and Alma Evelyn Hardin Mann, apparently were doting parents who made sure their children heard plenty of music. Bonnie recalls, "The earliest memories I have are of mama singing while she went about her work, or daddy sitting with one or two of us on his knee while he sang to us, bouncing us in time. Later came the wonderful time when they would sit with us and tell of their childhood and people long dead and sing the songs their parents had sung. My daddy liked the humorous songs while my mama's beautiful voice gave us a ballad or a spiritual tune she had learned from her mother, and almost always a good story to go with it."

Bob was born December 20, 1943, and Bonnie October 23, 1944 and they married shortly after graduating from high school. Autumn was born in 1964, Tina in 1968, Heather in 1974, Wade in 1975, and Nick in 1979. While the family played music and sang for their own enjoyment for many years, it was not until after the last of the five children was born that they started performing regularly in public. Their first public performance was in 1983 at a meeting of the Pulaski County (Arkansas) Rackensack Society, and since that date they have sung at a number of folk festivals and also made a week-long appearance at the 1984 World's Fair in New Orleans. Their traditional repertoire is huge, consisting of approximately 250 numbers. Probably, Bonnie learned this song from her mother, Alma, but she no longer recalls the specific time when she first heard it. She says, "It seems like I've always known this old family song."

I Will Arise

COLLECTED BY W.K. McNEIL FROM THE WILLIAMS FAMILY, ROLAND, ARKANSAS, APRIL, 1986. MUSIC
AND LYRIC TRANSCRIPTIONS BY W.K. McNEIL.

Come, thy fount of every blessing,
Tune thy heart to sing thy praise.
Dreams of mercy never ceasing,
Call for songs of loudest praise.

CHORUS:
I will arise and go to Jesus,
He will embrace me in his arms.
In the arms of my dear Saviour
Oh, there are ten thousand charms.

Here I raise my songs and praises,
Hither by thy help I come,
And I hope that by thy good measure
Safely to arrive at home.

Jesus sought me when a stranger,
Wand'ring from the fields of God.
He did rescue me from danger,
Interposed his precious blood.

There Is A Happy Land

Generally titled "Happy Land," this song is sometimes attributed to Leonard P. Breedlove or to Andrew Young. It is entirely possible that neither man wrote the song but merely made arrangements of it. Breedlove was active from the 1840s to the 1860s and wrote the tune for "Mercy's Free," which appeared in the 1850 edition of the *Sacred Harp*. The 1971 edition of the *Original Sacred Harp* contains a note that the "air of 'Happy Land' came from the Hindoes, an attribution that is highly improbable, though not impossible.

The present text is from the singing of Almeda Riddle, Greers Ferry, Arkansas, and was collected in March 1983 by W.K. McNeil. For biographical information about Riddle, see the comments given in the notes on "Twilight Is Stealing."

There Is A Happy Land

COLLECTED BY W.K. McNEIL FROM ALMEDA RIDDLE, GREERS FERRY, ARKANSAS, MARCH, 1983. MUSIC AND LYRIC TRANSCRIPTIONS BY W.K. McNEIL.

There is a happy land, far, far away,
Where saints and angels stand, bright, bright as day,
Hear how they sweetly sing, worthy is our glorious King,
Loud let his praises ring,
Praise, praise for aye.

Come to that happy land, O come, come away,
And why will ye doubting stand, why yet delay?
O we shall joyful be when from sin and sorrow free,
Lord, we shall live, shall live with Thee, live,
live for aye.

Bright in that happy land beams every eye,
Kept by the Father's hand, love never dies,
Then shall His kingdom come,
Saints will share a glorious home,
We'll reign beneath the sun, reign, reign for aye.

Sons of Sorrow

This song, also known as "Mouldering Vine," first appeared in print in William Caldwell's *Union Harmony*, published in Maryville, Tennessee, in 1837 (though registered in the district of East Tennessee in 1834). About Caldwell little is known beyond the fact that he was a singing-school teacher by 1820. Apparently, he recorded this tune from oral tradition somewhere in east Tennessee. It is thought to be derived from an older secular song, "Banks of Inverary."

The present text was collected by W.K. McNeil from the singing of Almeda Riddle, Greers Ferry, Arkansas, in March 1983. For more information about Riddle, see the notes to "Twilight Is Stealing."

Sons of Sorrow

COLLECTED BY W.K. McNEIL FROM ALMEDA RIDDLE, GREERS FERRY, ARKANSAS, MARCH, 1983. MUSIC
AND LYRIC TRANSCRIPTIONS BY W.K. McNEIL.

Hail! ye sighing sons of sorrow;
Come learn with me your certain doom;
Learn with me what's your fate tomorrow
Dead and perhaps laid in the tomb!
See all nature fading, dying!
Silent, all things seem to pine;
Life from vegetation flying,
Brings to our mind the mouldering vine.

Lo! in yonder forest standing,
Those lofty cedars; see them nod!
Scenes of nature, how surprising!
But read, in nature, nature's God.
While the annual frosts is cropping
Leaves and tendrils from the trees,
So our friends are yearly dropping
We are but like to one of these.

Former friends, so oft I sought them,
Just to cheer my troubled mind!
Now they're all gone, like leaves of autumn,
Driven before the dreary wind.
What to me is autumn's treasure,
For I know no earthly joy?
Long time have I lost all youthful pleasure,
Time will health and youth destroy.

Hollow winds about me roaring,
Noisy waters 'round me rise,
I sit here my fate deploring,
With the tears fast streaming from my eyes.
But cease this trembling, this mourning, sighing,
Death can break this solemn gloom;
Then my spirit, fluttering, flying,
Will be borne beyond the tomb.

CHAPTER THREE

Children's Songs

Rockabye, Baby

A popular song by this title is based on a poem in *Mother Goose's Melody* (1765) which began "Hush-a-bye, Baby, on the tree top." In 1872 Effie I. Crockett Carlton (1857-1940) composed music for the lyrics and changed the opening words. She did not publish the song until 1884, and then used the pseudonym Effie I. Canning. A version of Carlton's song was recorded on Edison cylinder 4036 sometime between 1896 and 1899 by pioneer recording artist George P. Watson. The present song is not the same as the Carlton number but is obviously a variant. It was collected June 20, 1951, by Irene Jones Carlisle from Annie Cagle, Woolsey, Arkansas, who learned the song from her parents.

In its present form, the song appears in no other collection (those references in the biblio-discography are to the usual version of "Rock-A-Bye Baby"), but Carlisle says an Evelyn Kiser of Fort Smith, Arkansas, often heard her mother sing it. Carlisle says "its British origin is obvious." She may be correct, but it also is possible that the song comes from the European mainland instead. The weight of the evidence, however, seems to be on Carlisle's side because earlier commentors on the usual form of "Rock-A-Bye Baby" are of the opinion that it is an English lullaby. It may well be a song connected with a game, but if so, it has escaped the attention of compilers of game collections.

Annie Cagle, fifty-six years old at the time of collection, lived with her husband and mother on Sugar Mountain, near Woolsey. The family raised chickens and Mr. Cagle did occasional construction work to earn a living. Mrs. Cagle was born in Iconium, Missouri, and moved to Ozark, Arkansas, about 1910. The family later moved to Watalulu, Arkansas, and then to Fayetteville, Arkansas, in 1927. Carlisle noted that "Mrs. Cagle has a very fine memory for songs, and a strong, sweet voice."

Rockabye, Baby

COLLECTED BY IRENE JONES CARLISLE FROM ANNIE CAGLE, WOOLSEY, ARKANSAS, JUNE 20, 1951.
MUSIC TRANSCRIPTION BY MRS. EVELYN KISER. LYRIC TRANSCRIPTION BY IRENE JONES CARLISLE.

Rockabye, Baby, your cradle is green;
Father's a noble, and mother's a queen.
Sister's a lady, she wears a gold ring;
Brother's a drummer, he drums for the king.

I Bought Me A Cat

This song is known by a variety of titles including "I Love My Rooster," "I Had a Little Hen," "I Bought Me a Hen," "Barnyard Song," and "The Farmyard," among others. As the last two suggest, the piece features imitations of various farmyard animals. Generally the song is thought of as a children's number, and youngsters are its main audience, but occasionally it is performed by adults as a comic number.

Although this piece undoubtedly is old, its exact age is uncertain. In *Games and Songs of American Children* (1883) William Wells Newell places it in the "remote past" but fails to specify just how long ago that might be. If, as seems likely, Newell meant many centuries ago, then this is the oldest song of its type still sung, not only in the Southern mountains but anywhere else. That is if Newell is correct. Often, though, mistakes have been made in determining the age of anonymous songs, particularly by nineteenth-century scholars who, like Newell, always considered their collected material to be survivals of the long ago and usually the far away. Newell was a very thorough scholar, and it seems logical that if he had information that would definitely date the song he would have given it. In short, Newell's attribution of age may not be wrong, but it is somewhat suspect.

Several folksong collections state that this song is a variant form of "Old MacDonald Had a Farm." If that is true, then the song does not predate the early eighteenth century. It is generally accepted that "Old MacDonald Had a Farm" is derived from a song sometimes called "In Praise of a Country Life" that was written by Thomas D'Urfey (1653-1723) and first published in 1706. If "I Bought Me a Cat" is a variation on the D'Urfey song, then it could not predate 1706, which would make it at most 177 years old when Newell published his text, the earliest one now known. That would make the song old in 1883 but hardly qualifies it for the "remote past." Of course, it also is possible that Henry M. Belden and Arthur Palmer

Hudson are correct in their opinion—expressed in *The Frank C. Brown Collection of North Carolina Folklore* III, p. 172—that just the reverse is true, that "Old MacDonald Had a Farm" is a variation of the present song.

Almost every animal commonly found around a farmyard is part of this song, but hens and cats are usually the first to receive mention. The place or type of tree where the animals are kept varies somewhat, but, considering the range of possibilities, seems remarkably stable. Newell's text has "that tree," and he refers to another text that has "green bay-tree"—the latter still commonly used today while the former is rare. One must remember, though, that Newell's texts were mostly examples of "memory culture," something recalled by adults from their youth. This means there is the possibility that the recall was not accurate, and a phrase such as "that tree" might have been more specific. In most texts, the animals are kept under "yonder" or "yonder's tree," but some other unusual trees also are mentioned. These include the "bamberry tree" and "oneyers [which may be a word resulting from a misunderstanding of the word "yonder's"] tree." Occasionally, some place other than a tree is mentioned; for example, a Kentucky text has the animals kept on "Dando's lea." In several texts, a few people are mentioned besides the singer, usually a wife or a baby. In one text from Durham, North Carolina, the singer concludes with a stanza beginning "I bought me a Ford and my Ford pleased me," but verses like this are rare.

The present text is from the singing of Charles Cagle, Woolsey, Arkansas, and was collected June 11, 1951 by Irene Jones Carlisle. At the time, Cagle, a man of average height and build, was fifty-seven years old and possessed a "low, pleasant singing voice." A native of Texas, he came to Arkansas in 1916, living first at Ozark and then later moving to the vicinity of Fayetteville. He learned this song from his parents when he was a small boy and later taught it to several nieces and nephews. Apparently, Cagle was shy about his singing, but he did perform at a 1951 folk festival held at the University of Arkansas, Fayetteville. For obvious reasons, Cagle referred to this, and songs similar to "I Bought Me a Cat," as "pile-up" songs.

I Bought Me a Cat

COLLECTED BY IRENE JONES CARLISLE FROM CHARLES CAGLE, WOOLSEY, ARKANSAS, JUNE 11, 1951.
MUSIC TRANSCRIPTION BY MRS. HOWARD R. CLARK. LYRIC TRANSCRIPTION BY IRENE JONES CARLISLE.

Bought me a cat, and the cat pleased me;
Fed my cat on yonders tree;
Cat says "fiddle fee."

Bought me a hen, and the hen pleased me;
Fed my hen on yonders tree;
Hen says "shin-shack, shin-shack,"
Cat says "fiddle fee."

Bought me a hog, and the hog pleased me;
Fed my hog on yonders tree;
Hog says "grivly, gravly,"
Hen says "shin-shack, shin-shack,"
Cat says "fiddle fee."

Bought me a dog, and the dog pleased me;
Fed my dog on yonders tree;
Dog says "bow wow,"
Hog says "grivly, gravly,"
Hen says "shin-shack, shin-shack,"
Cat says "fiddle fee."

Bought me a sheep, and the sheep pleased me;
Fed my sheep on yonders tree;
Sheep says "baa baa,"
Dog says "bow wow,"
Hog says "grivly, gravly,"
Hen says "shin-shack, shin-shack,"
Cat says "fiddle fee."

Bought me a cow, and the cow pleased me;
Fed my cow on yonders tree;
Cow says "moo moo,"
Sheep says "baa baa,"
Dog says "bow wow,"
Hog says "grivly, gravly,"
Hen says "shin-shack, shin-shack,"
Cat says "fiddle fee."

Bought me a horse, and the horse pleased me;
Fed my horse on yonders tree;
Horse says "neigh, neigh,"
Cow says "moo moo,"
Sheep says "baa, baa,"
Dog says "bow wow,"
Hog says "grivly, gravly,"
Hen says "shin-shack, shin-shack,"
Cat says "fiddle fee."

Bought me a wife, and the wife pleased me;
Fed my wife on yonders tree;
Wife says "Honey, honey,"
Horse says "neigh, neigh,"
Cow says "moo moo,"
Sheep says "baa baa,"
Dog says "bow wow,"
Hog says "grivly, gravly,"
Hen says "shin-shack, shin-shack,"
Cat says "fiddle fee."

Bought me a baby, and the baby pleased me;
Fed my baby on yonders tree;
Baby says "Mama, Mama,"
Wife says "Honey, honey,"
Horse says "neigh, neigh,"
Cow says "moo moo,"
Sheep says "baa, baa,"
Dog says "bow wow,"
Hog says "grivly, gravly,"
Hen says "shin-shack, shin-shack,"
Cat says "fiddle fee."

CHAPTER FOUR

Songs for Social Occasions

Jennie Jenkins

It is generally believed that this song is derived from the game song "Miss Jennia Jones," presumably because the latter includes verses asking what color dress the protagonist is to be buried in. This may indeed be the song's origin, but if so, then the number has changed in spirit a great deal over time. The original story was a tale of young love thwarted by cruel parents, culminating in the girl's death. After this, the "color" verses appear, followed by a discussion of her burial, and the song concludes with an account of her ghost. In the game, when this verse ends the ring breaks up with the players letting out shrieks, and the one who is Miss Jennia Jones catches another player who then takes her place. There is nothing funereal about the reported versions of "Jennie Jenkins," and, while all texts focus on the color of the girl's dress, this emphasis doesn't seem to have anything to do with the wearing of mourning colors. Instead, the lyrics have become a joyous song of courting.

The earliest reported version of "Jennie Jenkins" is a text titled "Jane Jenkins" that was printed in the *Green Mountain Songster*, a book compiled in 1823 by a Revolutionary soldier from Sandgate, Vermont. This publication suggests that the song was popular during the latter half of the eighteenth century. Evidence from other sources indicates that it remained a favorite throughout the nineteenth century, at least in some parts of the United States. In 1921 Thomas Smith reported a version as sung by Bennett and E.J. Smith of Zionville, North Carolina, who claimed first to have heard the number over forty years earlier in Caldwell County, North Carolina. The Smiths further told the collector that the song was very popular just after the Civil War.

In 1952 Ray Browne collected a version of the song from Mrs. Martha Jane Snyder of Tucson, Arizona, who said she learned it in Alabama seventy years earlier, i.e., in 1882. Vermont collector Alice Brown recorded a version of the song in 1930 as performed by Mrs. Susan Chase, Bethel, Vermont. Mrs. Chase had learned the song during her childhood from an aunt but apparently had not performed it for some time. She was able to recall only two verses, both referring to the color blue, but was certain there were several others, all of which referred to other colors. Obviously, this was an example of "memory culture"—but also positive proof that "Jennie Jenkins" had been popular in Vermont a few decades earlier when Mrs. Chase was a child.

Blue seems to be the favorite color appearing in the song. Red, brown, green, black, purple and yellow also are frequently used; but white, which appears in the earliest known text (from Sandgate, Vermont), is much less common. Among published samples, gray appears only in the 1823 Vermont version, and that lyric also contains what seems to be a nonsense word repeated as a refrain, "Onere, Onere." Another Vermont singer, Mrs. Chase, sang this as "Oh, narrow, narrow," which may well be the intended phrase in the Sandgate lyric. However, one should be cautious in using Mrs. Chase's text as giving the "true report" of how the song was sung in Vermont at one time because she was a passive singer, admittedly recalling the song only for the benefit of the collector. In any case, "Onere, Onere" is found in no other extant version of the song.

While there is some variety in the colors referred to, the questions asked and the rhymes remain essentially the same from one text to another. The greatest variation occurs in the chorus, with almost every singer supplying a different refrain. These range from the relatively simple lines like "So buy me a tally wooley, aye, sir" of the Susan Chase text to the more complex "I'll buy me a turly whirly double lolly sookey juley / Salley katy double double row stick a beany / Wau ter ma rose, Jennie Jenkins" of the Zionville, North Carolina, variant.

In 1929 Bascom Lamar Lunsford published a version of the song (reportedly learned from Charles Edwards, Buncombe County, North Carolina) that differs from the one given here even though both texts supposedly come from the same source. It is generally true, however, that versions of songs Lunsford published in *30 and 1 Folk Songs* differ from those he published or performed later. Whether these changes represent conscious or unconscious alteration is unknown. Like all known versions of "Jennie Jenkins," the lyrics in both Lunsford texts focus solely on colors; but they are given as red, brown, and blue in the 1929 publication rather than the green, red, black, blue, brown arrangement found here. The chorus differs also, the 1929 text having "I'll buy me a tella walka bella silk / To wear with my robe / To go with my robe / Jinnie Jinkins." In neither the 1929 publication nor in this later text did Lunsford supply the date he obtained the song from Charles Edwards. A good guess, though, is that it was probably during the first decade of the twentieth century.

Jennie Jenkins

FROM THE SINGING OF BASCOM LAMAR LUNSFORD. MUSIC TRANSCRIPTION BY JOHN M. FORBES. LYRIC TRANSCRIPTION BY LOYAL JONES.

Will you wear green, oh my dear, oh my dear.
Will you wear green, Jennie Jenkins?
I won't wear green, it can't be seen.
I'll buy me a tally fally-i-zer

CHORUS:
I'll buy me a tally walker belt-o-silk,
to wear with my robe, to go with my robe,
Jennie Jenkins.

Will you wear red, oh my dear, oh my dear?
Will you wear red, Jennie Jenkins?
I won't wear red; it's the color of my head.
I'll buy me a tally fally-i-zer.

CHORUS:
I'll buy me a tally walker belt-o-silk,
to wear with my robe, to go with my robe,
Jennie Jenkins.

Will you wear black, oh my dear, oh my dear?
Will you wear black, Jennie Jenkins?
I won't wear black; it's the color of my back.
I'll buy me a tally fallyizer.

CHORUS:
I'll buy me a tally walker belt-o-silk,
to wear with my robe, to go with my robe,
Jennie Jenkins.

Will you wear blue, oh my dear, oh my dear?
Will you wear blue, Jennie Jenkins?
I won't wear blue; it's the color of my shoe.
I'll buy me a tally fallyizer.

CHORUS:
I'll buy me a tally walker belt-o-silk,
to wear with my robe, to go with my robe,
Jennie Jenkins.

Will you wear brown, oh my dear, oh my dear?
Will you wear brown, Jennie Jenkins?
Yes, I'll wear brown; I'll go uptown.
I'll buy me a tally fallyizer.

I'll buy me a tally walker belt-o-silk,
to wear with my robe, to go with my robe,
Jennie Jenkins.

Cindy

Most collectors commenting on this song say that it is derived from an antebellum minstrel show song, or more precisely that it is made up of song fragments that have become attached to the refrain of an antebellum song. Undoubtedly, this sort of accretion has taken place in the making of present versions of "Cindy," but it is by no means certain that the chorus to which these fragments have adhered originated in the minstrel show. As is noted elsewhere in this book, the relationship of early minstrel show songs and folk traditions is at best hazy. Portions of the song as known today were used as a play-party number, and that usage may well predate the minstrel show appearance. In any case, "Cindy" certainly predates the earliest reports of it by folksong collectors, dating only from the early twentieth century.

One of the songs that has contributed to some versions of "Cindy" is "The Roving Gambler"—itself derived from an older song, "Guerilla Man." One of the first reported collections, by Thomas Smith of Zionville, North Carolina, in 1915, contains a second verse beginning "She tuck me in the parlor / She fanned me with a fan" that is customarily associated with "Roving Gambler." That element is missing from most of the more recently collected versions of the song. Also absent from most recent reports of "Cindy" are lyrics usually associated with "Rye Whiskey," as, for example, these lines collected in Alliance, North Carolina, in 1927: "Beefsteak when I'm hungry / Gravy when I'm dry / Pretty little girl to love me / And heaven when I die." The most stable elements in the song are the chorus and the verses describing visits to Cindy's house. Also very common is the verse beginning "I wish I was an apple."

"Cindy" is popular as a fiddle and banjo instrumental as well as a vocal number. It has also appeared frequently on commercial recordings, being recorded by the Hillbillies, Clayton McMichen and Riley Puckett, the Blue Sky Boys, and Roy Acuff, among others.

Undoubtedly these performances helped keep the song alive, though it certainly would have survived without them. The present text is from the singing of Bascom Lamar Lunsford (1882-1973). Lunsford was known as the Squire of South Turkey Creek (a section of his home community of Leicester, North Carolina) and was a noted collector of Appalachian ballads and folksongs. He stated that he heard this song at parties when he was a boy. His version of "Cindy" is one of the longest yet reported.

Cindy

FROM THE SINGING OF BASCOM LAMAR LUNSFORD. MUSIC TRANSCRIPTION BY JOHN M. FORBES. LYRIC TRANSCRIPTION BY LOYAL JONES.

Cindy stole a punkin,
She toted it to town.
She saw a cop a-comin'
And she throwed that punkin down.

CHORUS:
Git along home, Cindy, Cindy,
Git along home.
Git along home, Cindy, Cindy.
I'll marry you someday.

She led me to the parlor,
She cooled me with her fan.
She swore that I was the prettiest thing
In the shape of mortal man.

CHORUS:
Git along home, Cindy, Cindy,
Git along home.
Git along home, Cindy, Cindy.
I'll marry you someday.

I wish I was an apple
A-hangin' in a tree.
Every time my sweetheart passed
She'd take a bite of me.

CHORUS:
Git along home, Cindy, Cindy,
Git along home.
Git along home, Cindy, Cindy.
I'll marry you someday.

She told me that she loved me,
She called me sugar-plum.
She throwed her arms around me.
I saw my time had come.

CHORUS:
Git along home, Cindy, Cindy,
Git along home.
Git along home, Cindy, Cindy.
I'll marry you someday.

Cindy got religion;
She shouted all around.
She got so full of glory,
She broke the preacher down.

CHORUS:
Git along home, Cindy, Cindy,
Git along home.
Git along home, Cindy, Cindy.
I'll marry you someday.

Cindy got religion,
She got it once before.
But when she heard this old banjo,
She's the first one on the floor.

CHORUS:
Git along home, Cindy, Cindy,
Git along home.
Git along home, Cindy, Cindy.
I'll marry you someday.

I wish I had a needle and thread
As fine as I could sew,
And a thimble from Baltimore
To make that needle go.

CHORUS:
Git along home, Cindy, Cindy,
Git along home.
Git along home, Cindy, Cindy.
I'll marry you someday.

I wish I had a needle and thread,
As fine as I could sew,
I'd sew the girls to my coattail
And down the road I'd go.

CHORUS:
Git along home, Cindy, Cindy,
Git along home.
Git along home, Cindy, Cindy.
I'll marry you someday.

Old Joe Clark

This melody is popular both as an instrumental and as a folksong. When used as an instrumental, it seems to be about equally popular as a banjo and a fiddle number. Its history has not been thoroughly traced, though it must be fairly old: it is reported as early as the 1840s in England and is almost certainly older—perhaps considerably more ancient. In *The American Play-Party Song* (p. 269), B.A. Botkin makes a not-altogether-convincing argument that portions of the song are derived from Albert Gordon Green's 1822 poem "Old Grimes." It seems more likely that the song is of English origin, especially since the earliest known reference, in James O. Halliwell-Phillipps's *The Nursery Rhymes of England* (1842), is from that country.

There is no doubt that even in the 1840s the song existed in the oral tradition of adults as well as children. For example, it was popular at an early date as a play-party song and, according to tradition, was a regular party game with fixed and definite figures. However, I have only been told that such a game existed; I have yet to find anyone who can tell me exactly how the game was structured. That is not too surprising because play-parties are now dead as a traditional activity—the last non-revival one known to me in the Ozarks having occurred in 1956. I am not aware of any traditional play-parties occurring in Appalachia even that recently. But Vance Randolph, who collected a version of "Old Joe Clark" in 1927 when play-parties were still a common traditional entertainment in the Ozarks, noted that the "game as I have seen it played is a wild medley of figures from other games, and the fact that the same tune is played by fiddlers at the square dances still further complicates matters. Occasionally some gifted player, with a shrill whoop to attract attention to himself, executes a sort of jig or breakdown, while the chorus is sung loudly by the other dancers who gather about him. And I have attended two parties in which all figures were dispensed with, and the players simply paired off and danced about in couples—a crude imitation of the 'round' dances introduced by the tourists, except that there was no music save the singing of the players." (*Ozark Folksongs*, III, p. 324.)

Although hundreds of texts have been recorded of "Old Joe Clark," it is unlike many folksongs in that the title seems to remain unchanged from version to version. One possible explanation for this situation is that "Old Joe Clark" is relatively simple and thus easy to recall, but in some instances the title is retained because the singers and musicians believe it refers to an actual person that they knew. Speaking about versions of this piece collected in eastern Kentucky, Leonard Roberts says: "I wonder if it could have a specific source or individual adaptation. For instance, when I was teaching folklore and collecting in southeast Kentucky, many students from Clay County declared that the song originated in that county. They related that an old Negro banjo picker by the name of Joe Clark became an institution of folk music by making up dance pieces and by serving as the subject of pieces made up on him. 'Old Joe Clark' they said was the most popular one on him." (*In the Pine*, p. 290).

Only slightly less stable than the title is the tune, though there are a few variants that wander pretty far from the norm. The most divergent examples are ones reported by Marion Thede from Oklahoma (p. 129, no. 2) and by Ira Ford (p. 121). These two are so different from the usual tune that it is possible they are unrelated. A version collected in Missouri by Vance Randolph (*Ozark Folksongs*, III, p. 324) has for its verses the tune usually associated with "Cindy," which is not too surprising since many versions of the two songs share a large number of verses. Indeed, the lyrics of "Old Joe Clark" are its least stable element, probably for the reasons suggested by Alan Jabbour in his notes to the LP *American Fiddle Tunes from the Archive of Folk Song*. Jabbour maintains that the verses "vary greatly only because the spirit of nonsense encourages conscious variation, addition, and deletion."

The most commonly encountered verses of "Old Joe Clark" are those describing visits to Clark's house or Clark's character or his possessions. The protagonist is, in some versions, a vicious man who even kills people but more often he is depicted as a local character. In part, this may be because many singers believe Clark is a real person—even a former member of their community or region—or it may be that it is easier to make up verses about someone who is considered a bit eccentric.

"Old Joe Clark" is traditional primarily in the South, and most people commenting on the song refer to it as Southern. But it also is found outside the South, as shown by Sam Bayard's Pennsylvania collection, which, though a compilation of fiddle tunes, includes one verse for this song. The seemingly greater popularity of "Old Joe Clark" in the South may reflect nothing more than heavier folksong collecting in the region.

The version given here is from the singing of Bradley Kincaid, known for field collecting expeditions during which he gathered traditional ballads and songs that he later incorporated into his act. Kincaid recorded the song in Chicago on October 8, 1930, for the Brunswick-Balke-Collender Company, this version being released on The Brunswick and Conqueror label. He was convinced that "Old Joe Clark" referred to a real person who lived in Manchester, Kentucky, and was killed by his own son. Kincaid told D.K. Wilgus that "Clark was a notorious character. He carried a long knife down the back of his neck all the time so that he could reach it and get it quickly. The Betty Brown that is mentioned in the song was living with Joe by force. One day Joe's hogs got out and got into the cornfield of his son on the adjoining farm. The son got his shotgun and killed Old Joe, which was the very thing that the girl (Betty Brown) wanted so she could get away from him."

Old Joe Clark

FROM THE SINGING OF BRADLEY KINCAID. MUSIC TRANSCRIPTION BY JOHN M. FORBES. LYRIC
TRANSCRIPTION BY LOYAL JONES.

Now I've got no money,
I've got no place to stay,
I've got no place to lay my head,
And the chickens a-crowin' for days.

Fare you well, old Joe Clark,
Fare you well I say.
Fare you well, old Joe Clark,
I'm goin' away to stay.

I wish I had a nickel,
I wish I had a dime.
I wish I had a pretty little girl
To kiss her and call her mine.

Fare you well, old Joe Clark,
Fare you well I say.
Fare you well, old Joe Clark,
I'm goin' away to stay.

I don't like that old Joe Clark,
I'll tell you the reason why.
He goes about the country
A-stealin' good men's wives.

Fare you well, old Joe Clark,
Fare you well I say.
Fare you well, old Joe Clark,
I'm goin' away to stay.

I went down to old Joe Clark's,
I did not mean no harm.
He grabbed his old forty-four
And shot me through the arm.

Fare you well, old Joe Clark,
Fare you well I say.
Fare you well, old Joe Clark,
I'm goin' away to stay.

Old Joe Clark's a mean old dog,
I'll tell you the reason why.
He tore down my old rail fence,
So his cattle could eat my rye.

Fare you well, old Joe Clark,
Fare you well I say.
Fare you well, old Joe Clark,
I'm goin' away to stay.

I went down to old Joe Clark's,
I found old Joe in bed.
I stuck my finger in old Joe's eye,
And killed old Joe stone dead.

Fare you well, old Joe Clark,
Fare you well I say.
Fare you well, old Joe Clark,
I'm goin' away to stay.

I wouldn't marry that old maid,
I'll tell you the reason why.
Her neck's so long and stringy
I'm afraid she'll never die.

Fare you well, old Joe Clark,
Fare you well I say.
Fare you well, old Joe Clark,
I'm goin' away to stay.

I went down to Dinah's house,
She was standin' in the door.
With her shoes and stockings in her hand,
And her feet all over the floor.

Fare you well, old Joe Clark,
Fare you well I say.
Fare you well, old Joe Clark,
I'm goin' away to stay.

Yonder sits a turtle dove,
Sitting on yonder pine.
You may weep for your true love
And I shall weep for mine.

Fare you well, old Joe Clark,
Fare you well I say.
Fare you well, old Joe Clark,
I'm goin' away to stay.

Old Joe Clark's a mighty man.
What will it take to please him?
A good old bottle of apple jack
And Betty Brown to squeeze him.

Fare you well, old Joe Clark,
Fare you well I say.
Fare you well, old Joe Clark,
I'm goin' away to stay.

Cluck Old Hen

The most popular title for instrumental versions of this tune is "Cacklin' Hen," but it also is commonly called "Old Hen Cackled" or "Cluck Old Hen" and, less commonly, "The Old Hen Cackled and the Rooster's Going to Crow," "Hen Cackle," "Cackling Pullet," "Cluckin' Hen," and "Cacklin' Hen and Rooster Too." Vocal versions of the song are usually called "Cluck Old Hen," though other titles occasionally are used. It is, and apparently has been for at least seventy-five years, popular as both a fiddle and a banjo tune.

While the piece is more common as an instrumental, it would be inaccurate to say that the vocal version is rare. The lyrics seem to be of the "floating verse" type (i.e., lyrics found in many songs and seemingly fitting all equally well), but they apparently do not occur in other songs. Almost always the verse "Old hen cackled, cackled in the lot / Last time she cackled, cackled in the pot" is included. Sometimes that is the only verse sung in an otherwise instrumental number.

Around the turn of the century America saw a spate of songs imitating the sounds of chickens or other rural animals. Possibly the best known of these is Joseph M. Daly's 1910 "Chicken Reel," a number still popular with fiddlers. It is likely that "Cluck Old Hen" dates from the same era, but some fiddlers I have talked with over the years say they heard from oldtimers that the tune was played in the late nineteenth century. Possibly it is not even of American origin, but is derived instead from a tune that originated in the British Isles. This possibility is heightened by the existence of a vaguely reminiscent melody in George Petrie's *The Complete Petrie Collection of Ancient Irish Music* (1903-1906). But until better and more extensive evidence is available, such an attribution remains little more than speculation. For the time being, all one can say with certainty is that the origin of this number is unknown.

Throughout the history of vaudeville, and probably earlier, a number of performers specialized in animal imitations. One such was a man, probably from Fort Smith, Arkansas, known as Barnyard Steve. During the 1920s and early 1930s he appeared on several Arkansas radio stations, and in 1929 he made a record for Okeh that is of interest for a number of reasons. One side features a tune called "Arkansas Bill Green," which is possibly the first commercially recorded example of a mouthbow solo. According to Steve's spoken introduction, the title refers to a certain kind of square dance that in Arkansas is, or was, called "Bill Green." The other side, "Out on the Farm," features Steve doing various barnyard imitations. A song like "Cluck Old Hen" would have been made to order for such a performer, and it is quite likely that the vaudeville stage or some other form of popular entertainment played a large but yet undocumented part in popularizing vocal versions of this number.

Of the various titles associated with "Cluck Old Hen," without doubt the most unusual is "Knock-Kneed Nanny and Fare-Thee-Well," the name used by the late fiddler Buddy Thomas of Emerson, Kentucky. In comparison with Thomas's title, "Cacklin' Pullet" by the Tennessee Ramblers is quite commonplace. Although the title of Fiddlin' John Carson's "The Old Hen Cackled and the Rooster's Going to Crow" is not particularly unusual, he plays in a unique style. His version is performed relatively slowly, making it sound more like a parlor piece than a dance tune. If the title is a fair indication, the "Cackling Hen Blues" recorded by unidentified artists on an unissued Okeh 78 is a unique rendition of the tune, the only one transforming the piece into a bluesy number.

The version of "Cluck Old Hen" given here was recorded by Loyal Jones in Berea, Kentucky, from the singing of Sheila Adams Barnhill, October 27, 1979. Barnhill, who at the time was in her mid-twenties, is the niece of folksinger Dellie Norton, one of several well known traditional performers from Sodom, North Carolina. There is no indication of Barnhill's source for this song, but it—like most of her repertoire—probably was learned from one of her family, seven generations of which have been active in singing old ballads and folksongs. While her text is not particularly lengthy, it is longer than most reported versions of "Cluck Old Hen."

Cluck Old Hen

COLLECTED BY LOYAL JONES FROM SHEILA ADAMS BARNHILL IN BEREA, KENTUCKY, OCTOBER 27,
1979. MUSIC TRANSCRIPTION BY DAN BRACKIN. LYRIC TRANSCRIPTION BY W.K. McNEIL.

My old hen's a good ol' hen,
She lays eggs for the railroad men,
Sometimes one and sometimes two,
Sometimes enough for the whole dang crew.

Cluck old hen, cluck and sing,
Ah-ain't laid an egg since way last spring.
Cluck old hen, cluck and squall,
Ah-ain't laid an egg since way last fall.

My old hen's a good ol' hen,
She lays eggs for the railroad men,
Sometimes one and sometimes ten,
And that's enough for the railroad men.

Cluck old hen, cluck a lot,
Next time you cluck you're gonna cluck in the pot.
Cluck old hen, cluck and squall,
Ah-ain't laid an egg since way last fall.

Cluck old hen, cluck and squall,
Ah-ain't laid an egg since way last fall.
Cluck old hen, cluck and sing,
Ah-ain't laid an egg since way last spring.

Pretty Little Pink

Although most folksong scholars agree that this song dates back only to the Mexican War (1846-1848), the earliest reported text, from eastern Tennessee in 1883, contains the following lyric:

> *I've got my knapsack on my back,*
> *My musket on my shoulder,*
> *To march away to Quebec Town,*
> *To be a gallant soldier.*

This reference to Quebec suggests the possibility that the song originated during the French and Indian War (1754-1763), or about a century earlier than is generally believed. Some other texts mention New Orleans and thus make a War of 1812 origin plausible. It is, of course, also possible that the song predates all three wars and harks back to an as yet undiscovered *urform*. This seems to be what Ben Botkin is suggesting in *The American Play-Party Song*, p. 71, when he says the song "presents a curious example of a dance song which has been converted into a soldiers' marching song, with Mexican War references, and then taken back into dance usage, war references and all."

Whether dating from the Mexican War or earlier, the song definitely was used in play-parties and featured three sets of lyrics. Those beginning "my pretty little pink" or "my pretty little miss" or "my blue-eyed gal" (often with the command to "fly around" preceding the statement) and another set beginning "coffee grows on white oak trees" are the most common, while a third beginning "I'll put my knapsack on my back" is only slightly less popular. Often, only two of these lyrics appear, and occasionally only one. Of these three elements, the stanza beginning "coffee grows on white oak trees" seems to be of most recent vintage and may, as Botkin suggests in *The American Play-Party Song*, p. 94, represent a borrowing from another song of more recent origin than that containing the other two most frequently occurring stanzas.

The present text is from the singing of Doc (his real first name) Hopkins, a native of Harlan County, Kentucky, and is taken from a tape he made in the late 1960s or early 1970s. Hopkins (1900-1988), a guitarist and vocalist, spent two decades as a performer on the WLS National Barn Dance. During the early part of his stay at the Chicago station, he was associated with the Cumberland Ridge Runners, a string band led by John Lair and featuring musicians mainly from the Mt. Vernon-Renfro Valley, Kentucky area. Later he was purely a solo act.

Prior to his arrival at WLS, Hopkins spent ten years working with medicine shows. Although he was a professional performer who was at one time quite popular, Hopkins made few commercial recordings, possibly because the management of the radio station discouraged such activity by its performers. Hopkins was one of the most traditional Barn Dance performers, his repertoire leaning heavily towards folksongs and ballads. "Pretty Little Pink" he learned from fellow performer Bradley Kincaid, another one-time National Barn Dance artist who also had a very traditional repertoire. Kincaid, in turn, learned it from a third, very traditional performer, Scott Wiseman. Just where Wiseman acquired the song is unknown, but it may well have been learned from his own family. The song is in the folk tradition of that region of western North Carolina where Wiseman lived.

Pretty Little Pink

FROM THE SINGING OF DOC HOPKINS. MUSIC TRANSCRIPTION BY DAN BRACKIN. LYRIC TRANSCRIP-
TION BY W.K. McNEIL.

> Lord, Lord, my pretty little pink,
> Lord, Lord, my pretty little pink,
> I'm a-goin' away to stay.
>
> Well, I reckon you think my pretty little pink
> That I can't live without you,
> But I'll let you know before I go
> That I care but a little about you.
>
> Fly around my pretty little pink,
> Fly around my daisy,
> Fly around my pretty little pink,
> You almost drive me crazy.

Coffee grows on white oak trees,
The river flows with brandy.
The rocks on the hills all covered with gold,
And the girls all sweeter than brandy.

So, fly around my pretty little pink,
Fly around my daisy,
Fly around my pretty little pink,
You almost drive me crazy.

Well, everytime I go that road
It looks so dark and cloudy.
Everytime that I see little pink
I always tell her "howdy."

So, fly around my pretty little pink,
Fly around my dandy,
Fly around my pretty little pink,
I don't want none of your candy.

Drink 'er Down

This lively drinking lyric is a variant of the song Arthur Loesser includes in his *Humor in American Song*, pp. 304-5. As Loesser indicates, the song is known both as "Bingo" and "Here's to Good Old Yale, Drink it Down, Drink it Down," with the latter being the earlier title. This song dates from 1853 and probably was written by a Julien Carle, about whom nothing else is known, but the lyrics usually heard today date from an 1861 arrangement by H.T. Bryant. Today the refrain of "Balm of Gilead" is used commonly for the song, but Bryant featured a tune strongly reminiscent of "The Old Gray Mare." Neither of those melodies is used in the present version, which may suggest nothing more than that great melodic variation has occurred over a century of transmission through folk tradition. On the other hand, it could mean that the song was in existence prior to the 1853 Yale song.

The text given here was recorded March 21, 1951, by Irene Jones Carlisle from the singing of Rachel Henry and Frances Oxford, Spring Valley, Arkansas. Henry and Oxford were sisters both in their seventies at the time of collection. They both learned this song as small children from the singing of their stepfather. According to the collector, the two women greatly enjoyed singing this, and all of the other songs in their vast repertoires. Even so, despite their delight in this song, Henry and Oxford both disapproved of drinking.

Drink 'er Down

COLLECTED BY IRENE JONES CARLISLE FROM RACHEL HENRY AND FRANCES OXFORD, SPRING VALLEY, ARKANSAS, MARCH 21, 1951. MUSIC TRANSCRIPTION BY MRS. HOWARD R. CLARK. LYRIC TRANSCRIPTION BY IRENE JONES CARLISLE.

Oh, she's Number One; drink 'er down, boys,
Drink 'er down.
Oh, she's Number One; drink 'er down, boys,
Drink 'er down.
Oh she's Number One, and we'll all have fun;
Drink 'er down, boys;
Drink 'er down.

Oh, she's Number Two; drink 'er down, boys,
Drink 'er down.
Oh, she's Number Two; drink 'er down, boys,
Drink 'er down.
She's Number Two, and we're all in a crew;
Drink 'er down, boys;
Drink 'er down.

Oh, she's Number Three; drink 'er down, boys,
Drink 'er down.
Oh, she's Number Three; drink 'er down, boys,
Drink 'er down.
Oh, she's Number Three, and we're all on a spree;
Drink 'er down, boys;
Drink 'er down.

Oh, she's Number Four; drink 'er down, boys,
Drink 'er down.
Oh, she's Number Four; drink 'er down, boys,
Drink 'er down.
Oh, she's Number Four, and we're all on the floor;
Drink 'er down, boys;
Drink 'er down.

Oh, she's Number Five; drink 'er down, boys,
Drink 'er down.
Oh, she's Number Five; drink 'er down, boys,
Drink 'er down.
Oh, she's Number Five, and we're all yet alive;
Drink 'er down, boys;
Drink 'er down.

Oh, she's Number Six; drink 'er down, boys,
Drink 'er down.
Oh, she's Number Six; drink 'er down, boys,
Drink 'er down.
Oh, she's Number Six, and we're all in a fix;
Drink 'er down, boys;
Drink 'er down.

Oh, she's Number Seven; drink 'er down, boys,
Drink 'er down.
Oh, she's Number Seven; drink 'er down, boys,
Drink 'er down.
Oh, she's Number Seven, and we'll all get to Heaven;
Drink 'er down, boys;
Drink 'er down.

Oh, she's Number Eight; drink 'er down, boys,
Drink 'er down.
Oh, she's Number Eight; drink 'er down, boys,
Drink 'er down.
Oh, she's Number Eight, and we can't walk straight;
Drink 'er down, boys;
Drink 'er down.

Oh, she's Number Nine; drink 'er down, boys,
Drink 'er down.
Oh, she's Number Nine; drink 'er down, boys,
Drink 'er down.
Oh, she's Number Nine, and we're all dressed fine;
Drink 'er down, boys;
Drink 'er down.

Oh, she's Number Ten; drink 'er down, boys,
Drink 'er down.
Oh, she's Number Ten; drink 'er down, boys,
Drink 'er down.
Oh, she's Number Ten, and we're all in the pen;
Drink 'er down, boys;
Drink 'er down.

Oh, she's Number Eleven; drink 'er down, boys,
Drink 'er down.
Oh, she's Number Eleven; drink 'er down, boys,
Drink 'er down.
Oh, she's Number Eleven, and we'll never get to Heaven;
Drink 'er down, boys;
Drink 'er down.

Oh, she's Number Twelve; drink 'er down, boys,
Drink 'er down.
Oh, she's Number Twelve; drink 'er down, boys,
Drink 'er down.
Oh, she's Number Twelve, and we'll all go to hell;
Drink 'er down, boys;
Drink 'er down.

CHAPTER FIVE

Songs of Work

Roll On, John / Poor Rail Road Boys

This variant of the song usually known as "Roll On, Buddy" or "Nine-Pound Hammer" has been, as the bibliographic notes indicate, sparsely reported in folksong collections. One suspects, though, that it is more popular in folk tradition than the printed record reveals. The prominence of versions of "Nine Pound Hammer" has tended to obscure somewhat the "roll" variants of the song, such as "Roll On, John," and the "non-hammer" variants, such as "Poor Rail Road Boys." Much of the popularity of the "hammer" versions is due to frequent commercial recordings, including very successful ones by Merle Travis and Lester Flatt and Earl Scruggs. Despite its greater visibility, the "hammer" variant doesn't appear to be any older than the "roll" variant. Indeed, the latter, or a portion of it, appeared in print earlier. The first published song containing the phrase "nine pound hammer" can be found in E.C. Perrow's 1913 article "Songs and Rhymes from the South," while a song containing the sun reference common to the "roll" songs appeared in a 1912 Texas Folklore Society publication. Actually, the phrase "roll on, Johnnie" was sung in Texas in 1891.

During the early twentieth century, there were a number of other reports of the "roll" version of "Nine Pound Hammer." In 1915 Newman Ivey White received a fragment of the song from a Georgia source that contained this line: "Some o' these mornings, and 't won't be long / Capt'n gwine ta call me and I be gone." Probably about the same time—though because it is undated one can't be certain—a Mrs. O.L. Coffey of Shull's Mills, North Carolina, contributed to Frank C. Brown a song called "Some of These Days and It Won't Be Long." This title was taken from the number's first line, but the chorus had these lines: "Oh, boys don't roll so slow / When the sun goes down you'll roll no more." In 1924 Robert Winslow Gordon printed in *Adventure* magazine a collection of six work song fragments contributed by Charles Miller of

Waycross, Georgia, who had heard them in Southern railroad and construction camps. One of these included the following verses:

> *I looked at the sun, and the sun looked high,*
> *I looked at the boss, and the boss looked shy.*
>
> *And it's roll on, buddy,*
> *What makes you roll so slow?*
> *Your buddy is almost broke*
> *Down on the K.N.O.*
>
> *In a few more days, and that won't be long,*
> *Till the roll will be called, and I'll be gone.*

In 1927 Buell Kazee recorded "Roll On, John" for the Brunswick label, the first commercial recording of the "roll" variant of "Nine Pound Hammer." The words went:

> *Oh, roll on John, and make your time,*
> *For I'm broke and can't make mine.*
>
> *Oh, I dreamed last night, oh, Lou was dead,*
> *With her apron string tied around her head.*
>
> *Oh, who's been here since I've been gone?*
> *It's old Aunt Jenny with her night cap on.*
>
> *Oh, up to my chin, and under my nose,*
> *Where a many of a quart and a gallon goes.*
>
> *Oh, roll on John; don't roll so slow,*
> *When the sun goes down, we'll roll no more.*

In 1946 collector Margot Mayo recorded a version of "Roll On, John" from Kentucky folk musician Palmer Crisp and deposited it in the Library of Congress Archive of American Folk Song. Crisp's version was learned by Ralph Rinzler, who brought the song to the attention of the urban folksong revival when he recorded it in 1964 with The Greenbriar Boys.

A major point of debate concerning this song is whether it originated among blacks or whites. Some of the earliest references are from African-American informants, but several also are from whites. So, the most logical and, probably, most accurate position to take is to say that the song has undergone a long evolution in which both blacks and whites played some part. The two most stable elements are stanzas about the position of the sun and the lines about calling one's name, at which time the singer will be gone. These, however, are fairly common in both white and black work songs, so they provide no real evidence about the specific racial origins of the piece.

"Roll On, John" is from the singing of Buell Kazee, Winchester, Kentucky, and was recorded in 1972 by Mark Wilson. For biographical information about Kazee, see the notes for "Look Up, Look Down, That Lonesome Road." In a letter to folklorist Archie Green (printed in *Only a Miner*, p. 342), Kazee explained how he acquired "Roll On, John":

> It is among my first memories [meaning sometime between the years 1900-1910] and I have no idea how long before that it was sung. Like most of the songs which we knew it had come down with the heritage. It is connected with no historical event that I know. The tune follows the pattern of "Roll On Buddy" although the time and mood are radically changed. This I attribute to the old style of banjo playing which I and others did. All stanzas that I know of "Roll On John" were definitely sung with this song from my first memory, but I had never heard of "Roll On Buddy" in those early years. That probably was being sung over on some other creek. I heard it first in Corbin, Kentucky, about the time I was recording.

It is interesting to compare the text given here with the 1927 Kazee recording of "Roll On, John." The two versions are, of course, quite similar, but there is considerable rearrangement of verses. This may be surprising to some, considering that the song is relatively short, but it is not really that uncommon. The verse beginning "Oh, up to my chin, and under my nose" on the 1927 record is omitted from the 1972 text, and the other verses are rearranged. The first verse in 1927 becomes the last verse in 1972, and the last verse in 1927 is the first verse in the 1972 version; the positions of the second and third verses in 1927 are switched in 1972. Finally, the name Lou used in 1927 is expanded to Cora Lou in 1972. Whether these changes were intentional or merely the result of memory loss or some other unintentional reason cannot now be stated with certainty. They are, however, the kinds of changes that frequently occur in folksongs.

"Poor Rail Road Boys" was collected in April, 1941, by Theodore Garrison from Mrs. Zona Baker, Zack, Arkansas. At the time, Mrs. Baker was about sixty-five years old and the song almost certainly was learned from oral tradition because she was, according to Garrison, "almost illiterate." Apparently, she also considered the text she sang for Garrison only a fragment of the song because Garrison implies that Mrs. Baker knew there were several more verses. Mrs. Baker came from a family locally noted as traditional singers, and she had a huge repertoire, for she gave Garrison a sizeable number of songs. Garrison thought this was an unusual type of song for Searcy County (where Zack is located) and hypothesized that the song was introduced into the area "by migrant workers when the Missouri and North Arkansas railroad was being built there between 1900 and 1905."

Roll On, John

RECORDED IN 1972 BY MARK WILSON FROM THE SINGING OF BUELL KAZEE, WINCHESTER, KENTUCKY. MUSIC TRANSCRIPTION BY DAN BRACKIN. LYRIC TRANSCRIPTION BY LOYAL JONES.

Oh, roll on, John.
Don't roll so slow.
When the sun goes down,
You'll roll no more.

Oh, who's been here,
Since I've been gone?
It's old Aunt Jennie
With her nightcap on.

Oh, I dreamed last night,
Cora Lou was dead
With her apron string
Tied around her head.

Oh, roll on, John,
And make your time.
For I'm broke down,
And I can't make mine.

Poor Rail Road Boys

COLLECTED BY THEODORE GARRISON FROM MRS. ZONA BAKER, ZACK, ARKANSAS, APRIL, 1941. MUSIC
AND LYRIC TRANSCRIPTIONS BY THEODORE R. GARRISON.

Poor rail road boys ain't got no home;
He's here today, tomorrow gone.

I looked at the sun, and the sun was low.
I said to the boss man, "I must go."

O boss man, boss man, give me my time.
He clamped his hands and gave me a dime.

Oh, some of these days, and it won't be long,
My name'll be called and I'll be gone.

Reuben

This song is known under at least a dozen different titles, the most popular for the vocal versions being the one used here and "Reuben's Train" and "Old Reuben." "Train 45" is the title most often used for instrumentals. A text titled "Reuben's Train" in the *Frank C. Brown Collection of North Carolina Folklore* has three verses and a chorus containing the following lines: "A hundred miles / a hundred miles / a hundred miles from my home / You could hear the whistle blow / a hundred miles." This lyric suggests a relationship noted by other editors between this song and "900 Miles."

Brown's other text, which is from a black South Carolina informant, tells a story about Reuben getting drunk and going off to Mexico. It also contains the following lyric that reinforces the "900 Miles" connection: "When you hear dat whistle blow, blow / One hundred miles below." The song is popular in both black and white folksong traditions, a fact that has been overlooked by some authorities. For example, in one of the early published references to the song, a 1928 *New York Times Magazine* article by Robert Winslow Gordon, it is billed as "a mountain banjo song" titled "Old Reuben." But it definitely wasn't just a mountain tune, for in a 1931 *Journal of American Folklore* article Robert Duncan Bass recalled hearing the song sung by two Florence County, South Carolina, blacks in 1905, in the low country.

In 1959 Frank Warner collected a version of the song from Frank Profitt, Reese, North Carolina; Profitt later recorded essentially the same version for Sandy Paton of Folk-Legacy Records. Profitt told Warner this was one of the "oldest simple banjo tunes. Any mountain boy was excited when he learned to pick 'Old Reuben.' It was generally the first tune learned ... There are about fifty different verses to this, as everybody added them all along." Actually, no one has yet published a version anywhere near fifty verses in length. Profitt is probably correct, though, in stating that people constantly add to this song.

In *Long Steel Rail: The Railroad in American Folksong,* Norm Cohen distinguishes six basic types of this song. Type A consists of stanzas concerning Reuben, an engineer with a drinking problem and other unsavory habits. These versions usually begin with a verse similar to this: "Oh, you ought to been up town / when Reuben's train rode down / Lord, you could hear the whistle blow a hundred miles." In Type B the narrator pleads with his lover for a sign of affection, or he threatens to leave her. These versions contain an opening stanza such as the following: "If my woman says so / I'll railroad no more / I'll sidetrack my train and go home." Type C tells of a wanderer who either wants, or is trying, to get back home to his true love. It is characterized by stanzas such as this: "I'm walking down these ties with tears in my eyes / Trying to read a letter from my home." Type D deals with a conversation between a hobo and a tramp and contains verses similar to the following: "Oh, the hobo said to the bum, 'If you got any liquor I want some, / But I can't see my mamma this-a-way.'" Type E begins with a stanza telling the listener what to do "If I die a railroad man." Finally, Type F begins "Oh, the train's off the track," with the narrator worried about either getting home or getting a letter to his lover.

Obviously, there is a good deal of variation in reported versions of this song—so much, in fact, that most commentators have wondered if they were dealing with variants and versions of one song or of several once-independent songs. One detail showing a great deal of variation is the distance. One hundred miles most often is used, but distances of 90, 400, 500, 900, 1,000, and 10,000 miles also are found in some versions. The so-called folk revival may be primarily responsible for popularizing the "500 Miles" form of the song. Hedy West, a singer from Cartersville, Georgia, learned "500 Miles" from her grandmother and frequently performed it in concerts and eventually recorded it. Various groups, including the Kingston Trio, and Peter, Paul, and Mary, recorded West's version, and country singer Bobby Bare made the top ten on both the *Billboard* country and pop charts with his 1963 rendition of "500 Miles Away from Home."

Georgia musician Fiddlin' John Carson was the first artist to make a commercial recording of "Reuben." His August 27, 1924, recording for the General Phonograph Corporation titled "I'm Nine Hundred Miles from Home" also was the earliest known use of the phrase "900 Miles" as part of the title. It seems unlikely, though, that Carson was the first who actually used the term in the title. Woody Guthrie also played a role in disseminating the "900 Miles" variant of "Reuben." In April 1944, Guthrie made two recordings of the song, one under the title "900 Miles" and the other as "Railroad Whistle." They are clearly versions of the same song, but one, "Railroad Whistle," is a minor tune while the other is a major. This minor tune may have been written by Guthrie—a prolific songwriter—and the existence of this melody prior to his recording cannot be proven. In any case, it later became standard among revival performers who either acquired it directly from Guthrie's recording or indirectly from someone who had it from that source. The main argument against Guthrie's composition of the melody is that he rarely wrote original *melodies,* preferring instead to use some already existing traditional tune. It is, of course, possible that he changed his usual pattern in this instance.

The present text is from the singing of Bascom Lamar Lunsford, who claimed to have heard it "about 1898." He added that "it gives something about the origin of blues." Assuming that Lunsford is correct in his dating, then this is the oldest known form of the song. It also is interesting that he uses the distance of five hundred miles rather than the more common one hundred.

Reuben

FROM THE SINGING OF BASCOM LAMAR LUNSFORD. MUSIC TRANSCRIPTION BY JOHN M. FORBES. LYRIC TRANSCRIPTION BY LOYAL JONES.

The wind is from the east,
And the snow is from the north,
And I'm five hundred miles from my home.

She's standin' in the door,
Thinks she can hear that whistle blow.
She can hear the whistle blow five hundred miles.

If that train side-tracks,
I'll ride that freight train back.
I'll catch old Number Nine as she rolls by.

Oh my shoe's a-gettin' tore,
And my foot's a-gettin' sore.
I'll never leave my home anymore.

Oh them women up in town,
Say they'll chain Reuben down.
They'll chain Reuben down so low.

CHAPTER SIX

Comic Songs

Ol' Coon Dog

The lyrics of most folksongs are made up largely of floating stanzas. But "Ol' Coon Dog" seems to contain more such lyrics than normal—making the possibility of identifying this song even more complicated than usual with folksongs. Just about every text reported to date has a different title and set of lyrics. Among published versions, only the one reported by Leonard Roberts in *Sang Branch Settlers* has the same title as the present text. Yet its lyrics and tune are basically different from the song offered here, though the two versions do have the second verse in common. Various versions of "Ol' Coon Dog" contain verses usually associated with the songs "Liza Jane," "Cindy," "The Kicking Mule," "Old Rattler," "Possum Up a 'Simmon Tree," and "Whoa Mule." Lyrically, the most frequently found part of the song is the following verse: "Somebody stole my old coon dog / I wish they'd bring him back." While there also is considerable variation melodically between versions, the tune is more stable than the lyrics.

Because of the chorus used in the present text, some commentators might consider the earliest reported texts to be two sets of lyrics collected in Knott County, Kentucky, about 1902. Those two texts, both from the same informant, seem to be much closer to "The Kicking Mule," and thus are not really ancestors of the present item. Even so, this song definitely was known during the early years of this century. Paul Brewster recalled it as the first tune he learned to play on the parlor organ but he fails to say exactly when that was. Brewster was born in 1898 so he probably is referring to the first decade of the twentieth century. Perhaps the real ancestor is represented by three texts titled "The Squirrel," collected by Cecil Sharp in Kentucky and Virginia in 1917 and 1918. They share no verses in common with the present text but are closer to the Kentucky text reported by Roberts in *Sang Branch Settlers*. The *Frank C. Brown Collection of North Carolina Folklore* includes five texts under the title "Uncle Joe Cut Off His Toe" and six under the title "Possum

Up a 'Simmon Tree." The latter bears more similarity to the present text than does the former. Two further songs included in the Brown collection, "De Possum Am a Cunning Thing" and "The Raccoon Has a Bushy Tail," also show some textual similarities to "Ol' Coon Dog." The same applies to "Possum Up a Gum Stump," given in Vance Randolph's *Ozark Folksongs*.

Although the song cannot be traced back past the early twentieth century, it seems likely that "Ol' Coon Dog" either originated in the minstrel shows of the nineteenth century or was very strongly influenced by such songs. Certainly "The Kicking Mule," some verses from which are found in texts of "Ol' Coon Dog," has such associations. Also, "Old Rattler," a song whose history has not been adequately traced but is believed to derive from minstrel sources, evidently influenced some versions of the present song. Few versions give the dog a name, but those that do refer to him as "Ranger" or "Rattler." The latter name is used in a text collected by Sharp from Mrs. S.V. Cannady, Endicott, Virginia, August 22, 1918, the earliest version in which the dog is named.

The present version of "Ol' Coon Dog" is from the singing of Bradley Kincaid. He did not indicate where he learned the song, merely noting that it was an "old fiddle tune." Kincaid recorded the song October 8, 1930, in Chicago for the Brunswick-Balke Collender Company—the record itself issued as Brunswick 485. Verses three and four seem to be unique to Kincaid's version and may represent an intentional contribution on the singer's part. Still, one cannot be certain about such matters. Kincaid did some songwriting, but he also was known for intentionally seeking out traditional songs. These two verses are in the folk style, with lyrics that possibly were traditional with Kincaid's unnamed informant.

Ol' Coon Dog

FROM THE SINGING OF BRADLEY KINCAID. MUSIC TRANSCRIPTION BY JOHN M. FORBES. LYRIC
TRANSCRIPTION BY LOYAL JONES.

Once I had an old coon dog,
As blind as he could be.
But every night at supper time
I believe that dog could see.

CHORUS:
Whoa, mule I tell you,
Whoa, mule I say.
Tie a knot in that mule's tail
And he will run away.

Somebody stole my old coon dog.
I wish they'd bring him back
To run the big hogs over the fence
And the little ones thru the crack.

CHORUS:
Whoa, mule I tell you,
Whoa, mule I say.
Tie a knot in that mule's tail
And he will run away.

The devil's on the hillside
Settin' in the sun
Kickin' off back sticks
A havin' him some fun.

Turtle in the mill pond
Rootin' in the moss.
Devil's on the hillside
Swearin' he's a hoss.

Possum up a 'simmon tree
Raccoon on the ground.
The raccoon said you son of a gun
Shake them 'simmons down.

Possum up a gum stump
Raccoon in the holler,
Pretty gal at Massa's house
As far as she can waller.

Massa had an old coon dog
As blind as he could be.
He treed a possum up a black gum stump
I believe that dog could see.

Whoa, mule I tell you
Whoa, mule I holler.
Tie a knot in that mule's tail
An' he'll go thru the collar.

Watch that mule go roun' the hill,
Watch him how he sails,
Watch him how he shakes his ears
And how he shakes his tail.

Liza Up in the 'Simmon Tree

This is a version of "Liza Jane" which has blended with "Possum Up a 'Simmon Tree" and, like both of those songs, owes something to the minstrel show. Unfortunately, just how much of this song comes from nineteenth-century professional songwriters and how much is derived from folk sources has never been adequately traced. In the 1880s the minstrel show performer Eddie Fox published "Good Bye, Liza Jane" but took no credit for writing the song. He merely billed himself as the arranger. Later, in 1903, the prolific Tin Pan Alley composer Harry Von Tilzer published "Good-Bye, Eliza Jane," but that song in the then-popular "coon song" style bears no relation to Fox's song or to the various permutations of the folksong "Liza Jane." In 1917 Cecil Sharp collected a song called "Liza Anne" in Lee County, Kentucky, that shows definite blending of "Liza Jane" and "Possum Up a 'Simmon Tree." Even so, it corresponds only in the most tangential way to the present song. Far closer is a "Liza Jane" reported by Jean Thomas and published in her book *Devil's Ditties*. Interestingly, Thomas referred to the song as a ballad even though her text presents no real narrative.

There seem to be two basic types of this song. The first is distinguished by a chorus consisting of "Oh, little Liza, / little Liza Jane," repeated. The second is the song given here. Lyrics most often found in this type are those concluding "She died on the train," those beginning "I wish I had a needle and thread," those beginning "I went to see my Liza Jane, she was standing in the door," and those beginning "Her head is like a coffee pot." None of these verses, of course, is unique to "Liza Jane." Indeed, most are also sometimes associated with versions and variants of "Cindy" and "Old Joe Clark."

The present text is from the singing of Bradley Kincaid, who learned it from his father. Kincaid (1895-1989) was a professional entertainer who spent some time on the National Barn Dance and the Grand Ole Opry as well as a number of other country music shows. Unlike most of today's professional country musicians, Kincaid had a repertoire largely made up of traditional songs, several from his own family tradition. He also made many collecting trips into the southern Appalachians to record folksongs that he then used on his shows. Of this song Kincaid said, "When I wasn't more than four years old my father had me singing that for company and they'd just laugh."

Liza Up in the 'Simmon Tree

FROM THE SINGING OF BRADLEY KINCAID. MUSIC TRANSCRIPTION BY JOHN M. FORBES. LYRIC TRANSCRIPTION BY LOYAL JONES.

Liza up in the 'simmon tree, and the possum on the ground.
Possum said, "You son of a gun, shake them 'simmons down."

CHORUS:
Whoopee Liza, pretty little girl.
Whoopee, Liza Jane.
Whoopee, Liza, pretty little girl.
She died on the train.

Cheeks are like cherries,
Cherries like a rose.
How I like that pretty little girl,
Goodness gracious knows!

The old folks down in the mountains, grinding sugar cane,
Making barrels of molasses, for to sweeten old Liza Jane.

Whiskey by the gallon, sugar by the pound,
A great big bowl to put it in, and Liza to stir it around.

I went to see my Liza Jane, she was standing in the door,
Shoes and stockings in her hand and her feet all over the floor.

Her head is like a coffee pot, her nose is like the spout,
Her mouth is like an old fireplace with the ashes all raked out.

I wouldn't marry a poor girl, I'll tell you the reason why,
She'd have so many poor kinfolks, she'd make my biscuits fly.

The hardest work I ever done, was a-brakin' on a train,
The easiest work I ever done, was huggin' little Liza Jane.

The Tobacco Song

This song is another of those that may be more popular in tradition than published reports indicate. To date, it has only been collected from traditional sources in North Carolina, Tennessee, and Arkansas. The melody is derived from the hymn "Heavenly Union" or "Experience," a number first published in *Christian Harmony* or *Songster's Companion* (1805), compiled by Jeremiah Ingalls and printed in Exeter, New Hampshire. Although the most common title seems to be "Tobacco Union," the song also has appeared in published collections as "Talking with the Social Union." The exact age of the song has yet to be determined, though it clearly dates back to the nineteenth century. Vance Randolph's informant, Maggie Morgan, Springdale, Arkansas, said she learned it either in the late 1880s or early 1890s, and, to date, that is as far back as the song has been traced. All reported texts show greater lyric than melodic variation.

The present version was recorded March 9, 1951, by Irene Jones Carlisle from Rachel Henry, Spring Valley, Arkansas, who had learned it as a child in Brush Creek, Arkansas, a nearby community. Mrs. Henry knew many songs, including a number of Child ballads, and was a sister of Frances Oxford, another of Carlisle's informants. In her seventies at the time of collection, Mrs. Henry was a jovial woman who occupied some of her time as a local correspondent for the *Springdale News*. Most of the songs in her repertoire she learned from young people of the community during her childhood. Like her sister, Frances Oxford, she greatly enjoyed singing, and the two often sang together. Carlisle noted that "Mrs. Henry has a strong, unmusical voice, which is nevertheless pleasing because of her delight in singing. She often forgets parts of her songs but goes right on chanting an approximation of the story until she gets back on the track." By the word "story" Carlisle obviously meant "lyric" rather than "narrative." The reference in the fourth verse to "gathering sticks" is to snuff-dipping. "Snuff sticks" or brushes were made of durable, sweet twigs, such as those of the willow tree, and were used to bring the snuff up to the mouth and then swab the gums with the tobacco.

The Tobacco Song

COLLECTED BY IRENE JONES CARLISLE FROM RACHEL HENRY, SPRING VALLEY, ARKANSAS, MARCH 9, 1951. MUSIC TRANSCRIPTION BY MRS. HOWARD R. CLARK. LYRIC TRANSCRIPTION BY IRENE JONES CARLISLE.

Come, old and young, and hear me tell
How strong tobacco's smoke or smell;
Who loves to smoke their pipes so well
That for tobacco they would sell
Their rights in social union?

Sometimes the smoke and fumes will rise
Like morning mist toward the skies;
And woe unto him that has weak eyes,
Unless he takes to his heels and flies
From this tobacco union.

Sometimes in church, in church you'll view
Some persons there to spit and chew;
Spit on carpet, floor and pew,
Until it spreads a spot or two,
And sing of heaven-lie union.

The ladies they are sweet, 'tis true,
But they have learned to use it too.
Sometimes you'll see some five or six
Out in the woods a-gathering sticks;
The sticks are cut and swabs are made,
And in a group they all parade;
And it's now for slobberin' union.

And then the snuff-box is pulled out,
And with their sticks they dip it out;
They rub their teeth insides and out,
And smear their faces all about,
And talk of matrimony.

The Kicking Mule

According to published field collections, this lively song is known throughout the Ozarks and in North Carolina, Tennessee, Alabama, Mississippi, Texas, Indiana, Virginia, and Kentucky. But one suspects that it is even more widely known than the printed reports indicate. Surprisingly, it appears in only one collection from a Northern state, Paul Brewster's *Ballads and Songs of Indiana;* yet, despite the book's title, Brewster's collection was from the southwestern quarter of Indiana—an area settled primarily by people from North and South Carolina, Virginia, and Kentucky. In short, collecting folksongs there was virtually the same as collecting in the South. The reason it is surprising "The Kicking Mule" has not been reported from the North is that the song ultimately derives from the blackface minstrel shows which were for nearly four decades (1843-1883) the most popular form of American popular entertainment. Minstrel shows were hugely successful in the North, so a song derived from that source seemingly should be popular there.

The original of this song was titled "Simon Slick," and that is the name sometimes used even today. Probably the first printed version appeared in John M. Turney's *The Coons Around Our Block Songster,* issued in New York in 1879. It possibly predates the Turney printing because he doesn't claim authorship, and it appeared in several subsequent songbooks without an author's credit. These include *George S. Knight's Songs and Recitations* (1880), *Andy Collum's Latest and Best Banjo Songs* (1881), *John Walsh's Gems of the Emerald Isle Songster* (1881), and *Murphy and Mack's Jolly Sailor's Songster* (1883). Some collectors have thought the song had African-American origins, but that seems unlikely. Although its frequent appearances in minstrel songbooks is not irrefutable proof that the number originated on the minstrel stage, the fact that there are no reports predating the minstrel ones gives great credence to a minstrel origin. Furthermore, the piece smacks stylistically of nineteenth-century American popular theater—though it should be noted that the relationship between the latter and folk tradition has yet to be studied adequately.

Even though the song did not originate among black Americans, it certainly is sung by them. Most reported texts include references to the sleigh ride and use the name Simon Slick, usually in reference to the owner and often as the name of the mule itself. Neither of these traits, however, is exclusive to African-American versions of the song. Both white and black texts are similar in several ways. All make reference to the various feats accomplished by the mule while kicking, and most conclude with the animal kicking itself to death. Most reported texts are relatively short, consisting of four or fewer verses. The one cited by Herbert Shellans and the one given here are unusual in their length. The Shellans text is unique in that it has two choruses; most other versions of the song have the same chorus repeated at various intervals. The minstrel versions go to another extreme and have no chorus at all.

Several versions contain references to ethnic and cultural groups. For example, Brewster's A text speaks of "Chinamen" and "Mexicans" and black people. Few texts, however, make reference to the ethnic or racial background of the song's main characters. The chorus of Brewster's B text implies that Simon Slick is black. Shellans's text leaves nothing to implication, for it explicitly states that Simon Slick was a "German man."

At some point, "Simon Slick" took on various elements from "Liza Jane" and "Whoa Mule," and most versions collected in the past fifty years reveal this blending. This number also is quite popular as a banjo instrumental in which the musician rakes his fingers across the strings in a manner that imitates the sound of a braying mule.

The version included here is from the singing of Bradley Kincaid, who learned the song from his father. Under the title "Let That Mule Go Aunk! Aunk!" Kincaid recorded the song June 7, 1929, for the Starr Piano Company in Richmond, Indiana. This recording was released on the Gennett, Champion, Supertone, and Superior labels. The beginning lines, though not unique to this text, are far from common for the piece. More often, the song begins by talking about the man who owns the mule.

The Kicking Mule

FROM THE SINGING OF BRADLEY KINCAID. MUSIC TRANSCRIPTION BY JOHN M. FORBES. LYRIC
TRANSCRIPTION BY LOYAL JONES.

Listen to me and I'll sing you a song.
I'll sing it all to you,
Sing you a song about the kickingest mule
That ever you did see.

CHORUS:
Let that mule go Awnk, Awnk, Awnk, Awnk, Awnk.
Give that mule more hay.
Keep your seat Miss Liza Jane
And hold on to the sleigh.

Hitched him up early one morning
To take my gal a ride,
Kicked both hind feet over the shaves
And kicked her in the side.

CHORUS:
Let that mule go Awnk, Awnk, Awnk, Awnk, Awnk.
Give that mule more hay.
Keep your seat Miss Liza Jane
And hold on to the sleigh.

Kicked the wings off of a wild goose
The ears off of a frog,
Kicked the brindle cat upon top of the house
And swallowed a great big dog.

CHORUS:
Let that mule go Awnk, Awnk, Awnk, Awnk, Awnk.
Give that mule more hay.
Keep your seat Miss Liza Jane
And hold on to the sleigh.

Oh, hear them sleigh bells ringing,
The snow is falling fast.
I put this mule in harness
And got him hitched at last.

CHORUS:
Let that mule go Awnk, Awnk, Awnk, Awnk, Awnk.
Give that mule more hay.
Keep your seat Miss Liza Jane
And hold on to the sleigh.

Oh, Liza get your bonnet.
Come and take your seat.
Grab the board you're sitting on,
And kiver up your feet.

CHORUS:
Let that mule go Awnk, Awnk, Awnk, Awnk, Awnk.
Give that mule more hay.
Keep your seat Miss Liza Jane
And hold on to the sleigh.

And watch this mule a climbing,
For this ain't half a load.
Find a mule that's roomy,
And give him all the road.

CHORUS:
Let that mule go Awnk, Awnk, Awnk, Awnk, Awnk.
Give that mule more hay.
Keep your seat Miss Liza Jane
And hold on to the sleigh.

And don't get scared at nothing,
What you hear or see.
Liza, I'll stay with this mule,
And you must stay with me.

CHORUS:
Let that mule go Awnk, Awnk, Awnk, Awnk, Awnk.
Give that mule more hay.
Keep your seat Miss Liza Jane
And hold on to the sleigh.

Just see them snowflakes flying.
Lookout let him sail.
Watch them ears of his'n,
And see him wag his tail.

CHORUS:
Let that mule go Awnk, Awnk, Awnk, Awnk, Awnk.
Give that mule more hay.
Keep your seat Miss Liza Jane
And hold on to the sleigh.

Goin' to the preacher's,
Liza you keep cool.
Hain't got time to kiss you now.
I'm busy with this mule.

CHORUS:
Let that mule go Awnk, Awnk, Awnk, Awnk, Awnk.
Give that mule more hay.
Keep your seat Miss Liza Jane
And hold on to the sleigh.

Little grasshopper came flying around,
Came flying around the well.
This little mule gave him one good kick,
Grasshopper didn't feel so well.

CHORUS:
Let that mule go Awnk, Awnk, Awnk, Awnk, Awnk.
Give that mule more hay.
Keep your seat Miss Liza Jane
And hold on to the sleigh.

Took him down to the blacksmith's shop
Hitched him by himself.
He kicked both hind feet down his neck,
And kicked himself to death.

CHORUS:
Let that mule go Awnk, Awnk, Awnk, Awnk, Awnk.
Give that mule more hay.
Keep your seat Miss Liza Jane
And hold on to the sleigh.

The Arkansas Run

This song has about as many titles as there are locales where it is sung, and most versions include a place name in the title. The earliest known printing, however, lacks the place-name title, though some geographical details appear in the text. In 1841 the music publishing company Firth and Hall issued this piece under the title "Free Nigger" without lyricist or composer credits. The lack of specific attribution suggests the song was not new, and perhaps was even in the public domain. Conversely, it may mean that the publisher knew the persons responsible for writing it and deleted mention of them in order to avoid paying royalties. In this initial printing, "Virginia gals" are warned about "Carolina boys."

It would be almost seven decades before anyone reported the song from oral tradition. Then, in 1910, John Lomax included a lengthy version—actually a composite partly taken from other sources—titled "The Texian Boys" that he had from J.D. Mitchell of Victoria, Texas, who claimed to have learned it in 1868 while on a trail drive. Mitchell said he got the song from an "old Acadian" who "learned it from his 'pap,' and his father told him it originated in the days of the Texas Republic." If this statement is accurate, then it makes even more plausible the likelihood that the song predates 1841.

In the Lomax text, Louisiana girls are warned against Texas boys. In other reported texts, unspecified girls, Tennessee girls, Alabama girls, Missouri girls, West Virginia girls, Mississippi girls, Illinois girls, and young girls are warned against Cheyenne boys, the Tucky Ho Crew, Missouri boys, and, most frequently, Arkansas boys. Sometimes it is not girls from a specific region that are warned or men from a particular area they are warned against. Thus, in one form of the song girls are warned against "Mormon boys." Indeed, this song is known throughout much of the United States and is quite flexible. It can be—and often has been—used satirically against the people of any region or cultural group.

There is also great variation in descriptions of the bad things that will befall those who fail to heed the warning. Generally, some account of the type of clothing girls will be subjected to, the kind of housing that will be provided, and the type of food that will be available is given, the latter being the most frequently mentioned. A little less common are comments on the shabby physical treatment to which the women will be subjected.

The present text was recorded in 1944 by Theodore Garrison, as recalled from the singing of his father, Sam Garrison, Searcy County, Arkansas. Apparently, Mr. Garrison had known the song for a long time because his son says, "One of my earliest recollections is hearing this song sung by my father." Theodore Garrison was born in 1917, so he recalled hearing it in the early 1920s. Sam Garrison was born in 1887, taught for seventeen years, and spent the rest of his life as a farmer. The word "run" as used in this song refers to "the common run" or "average person."

The Arkansas Run

MUSIC AND LYRIC TRANSCRIPTION BY THEODORE R. GARRISON AS RECALLED FROM THE SINGING OF HIS FATHER, SAM GARRISON, SEARCY COUNTY, ARKANSAS, 1944.

> Come, all of you Missouri girls, and listen to my noise.
> Be careful how you court these Arkansas boys,
> For if you don't your portion will be
> Cold johnny cake and venison for supper you'll see.
> Cold johnny cake and venison for supper you'll see.

When they go a-sparking, I'll tell you what they wear:
Their old woolen coats all pitched in tar,
Their old straw hats, more brim than crown,
And their old ducking britches they've worn the year round.
Their old ducking britches they've worn the year round.

When they go a-sparking, they'll go out on the grass,
And there they'll halter up a wild bull calf.
They'll halter him up with a big, long rope,
And on their journey they will lope.
And on their journey they will lope.

When they get to their journey's end,
"Have you got art rope for to lend me, my friend?
For I am a-riding a wild bull calf,
And I want to stake him out upon the grass.
And I want to stake him out upon the grass."

When he comes in and you set him a chair,
The first thing he says is, "Daddy killed a bear."
The next thing he says, as he sits down,
Is, "Madam, ain't your johnny cake a-baking too brown?
Madam, ain't your johnny cake a-baking too brown?"

When they go to milk, they'll milk it in a gourd,
Set it in the corner, and cover it with a board.
Some get a little, and some get none.
And that's just the way of the Arkansas run.
And that's just the way of the Arkansas run.

Notes

This section opens with a list of basic reference books mentioned in the biblio-discographies for each song. Each song writeup itself is arranged in four parts:

- A. (Basic references) features those books from the Basic Reference list. Usually a song text of some length appears on the pages cited, but in some cases the reference is to a single stanza or relevant portion of a song.

- B. (Other references) has printed sources not in section A, including studies of individual songs or collections. The remarks about text length given under section A also apply here.

- C. (78 RPM records) includes albums as well as individual records.

- D. (LP and cassette recordings) includes both new releases and reissues of 78s. Determining the correct title of an LP often is difficult because record companies are inconsistent in their titling policies. For example, in some cases one title is given on the front of the album, a second one on the back, a third one on the side, and a fourth one on the record itself. In cases where a record has more than one title I have opted for the one given on the front cover of the record jacket, basing my decision on the wholly arbitrary opinion that the album is most likely to be catalogued under the cover title.

None of the sections should be construed as exhaustive lists of either publications or recordings dealing with an individual song. Instead, they are intended merely as a representative sampling of what is available; in most cases, the listed items could be greatly increased. Where nothing appears under a numbered section, I was unable to locate any relevant items in that category for the specific song.

Basic Reference Books

Abrahams and Foss
Abrahams, Roger D., and George Foss. *Anglo-American Folksong Style.* Englewood Cliffs, New Jersey: Prentice-Hall, Inc., 1968.

Abrahams and Riddle
Abrahams, Roger D. *A Singer and Her Songs: Almeda Riddle's Book of Ballads.* Baton Rouge: Louisiana State University Press, 1970.

Bayard
Bayard, Samuel P. *Dance to the Fiddle, March to the Fife: Instrumental Folk Tunes in Pennsylvania.* University Park and London: The Pennsylvania State University Press, 1982.

Belden
Belden, Henry M. *Ballads and Songs Collected by the Missouri Folk-Lore Society.* 2nd edition. Columbia: University of Missouri Press, 1955.

Botkin
Botkin, Benjamin A. *The American Play-Party Song.* 2nd edition. New York: Frederick Ungar Publishing Company, 1963.

Botkin (1949)
Botkin, Benjamin A. *A Treasury of Southern Folklore.* New York: Crown Publishers, 1949.

Botkin (1955)
Botkin, Benjamin A. *A Treasury of Western Folklore.* New York: Crown Publishers, Inc., 1955.

Botkin and Harlow
Botkin, Benjamin A., and Alvin F. Harlow. *A Treasury of Railroad Folklore.* New York: Crown Publishers, Inc., 1953.

Brewster   Brewster, Paul G. *Ballads and Songs of Indiana*. 1940. Reprint. New York: Folklorica, 1981.

Brown III   *The Frank C. Brown Collection of North Carolina Folklore. Volume 3. Folk Songs.* Edited by Henry M. Belden and Arthur Palmer Hudson. Durham: Duke University Press, 1952.

Brown V   *The Frank C. Brown Collection of North Carolina Folklore. Volume 5. The Music of the Folk Songs.* Edited by Jan Philip Schinhan. Durham: Duke University Press, 1962.

Browne   Browne, Ray B. *The Alabama Folk Lyric: A Study in Origins and Media of Dissemination.* Bowling Green, Ohio: Bowling Green University Popular Press, 1979.

Burton and Manning I Burton, Thomas G., and Ambrose N. Manning. *East Tennessee State University Collection of Folklore: Folksongs.* Johnson City: East Tennessee State University, 1967.

Burton and Manning II Burton, Thomas G., and Ambrose N. Manning. *East Tennessee State University Collection of Folklore. Volume 2. Folksongs.* Johnson City: East Tennessee State University, 1969.

Cazden   Cazden, Norman. *The Abelard Folksong Book.* New York: Abelard-Schuman, 1958.

Cazden, Haufrecht,   Cazden, Norman, Herbert Haufrecht, and
Studer   Norman Studer. *Folk Songs of the Catskills.* Albany: State University of New York Press, 1982.

Cohen and Seeger   Cohen, John, and Mike Seeger. *The New Lost City Ramblers Song Book.* New York: Oak Publications, 1964.

Cohen, N.   Cohen, Norm. *Long Steel Rail: The Railroad in American Folksong.* Urbana: University of Illinois Press, 1981.

Combs and Wilgus	Combs, Josiah H. *Folk-Songs of the Southern United States.* Edited by D.K. Wilgus. Austin: University of Texas Press, 1967.
Cox	Cox, John Harrington. *Folk-Songs of the South.* 1925. Reprint. New York: Dover Publications, Inc., 1967.
Davis	Davis, Arthur Kyle, Jr. *Folk Songs of Virginia: A Descriptive Index and Classification.* Durham: Duke University Press, 1949.
Flanders and Brown	Flanders, Helen Hartness, and George Brown. *Vermont Folksongs and Ballads.* 1931. Reprint. Hatboro, Pennsylvania: Folklore Associates, Inc., 1968.
Fuson	Fuson, Henry H. *Ballads of the Kentucky Highlands.* London: The Mitre Press, 1931.
Gainer	Gainer, Patrick. *Folk Songs from the West Virginia Hills.* Grantsville, West Virginia: Seneca Books, 1975.
Henry (1934)	Henry, Mellinger E. *Songs Sung in the Southern Appalachians.* London: The Mitre Press, 1934.
Henry (1938)	Henry, Mellinger E. *Folk-Songs from the Southern Highlands.* New York: J.J. Augustin, 1938.
Huntington	Huntington, Gale, ed. *Sam Henry's Songs of the People.* Athens and London: University of Georgia Press, 1990.
Jackson	Jackson, George Pullen. *Spiritual Folk-Songs of Early America.* 1937. Reprint. New York: Dover Publications, Inc., 1964.
Jones (1984)	Jones, Loyal. *Minstrel of the Appalachians: The Story of Bascom Lamar Lunsford.* Boone, North Carolina: Appalachian Consortium Press, 1984.
Jones (1988)	Jones, Loyal. *Radio's 'Kentucky Mountain Boy' Bradley Kincaid.* 2nd edition. Berea,

	Kentucky: Berea College Appalachian Center, 1988.
Leisy	Leisy, James F. *The Folk Song Abecedary.* New York: Bonanza Books, 1966.
Lomax and Lomax	Lomax, John A., and Alan Lomax. *Folk Song U.S.A.* 2nd edition. New York: The New American Library, Inc., 1975.
Lunsford and Stringfield	Lunsford, Bascom Lamar, and Lamar Stringfield. *30 and 1 Folk Songs from the Southern Mountains.* New York: Carl Fischer, Inc., 1929.
MacIntosh	MacIntosh, David S. *Folk Songs and Singing Games of the Illinois Ozarks.* Edited by Dale R. Whiteside. Carbondale: Southern Illinois University Press, 1974.
Morris	Morris, Alton C. *Folksongs of Florida.* 1950. Reprint. New York: Folklorica, 1981.
Owens (1950)	Owens, William A. *Texas Folk Songs.* Dallas: Southern Methodist University Press, 1950.
Owens (1983)	Owens, William A. *Tell Me a Story, Sing Me a Song: A Texas Chronicle.* Austin: University of Texas Press, 1983.
Raim and Dunson	Raim, Ethel, and Josh Dunson. *Grass Roots Harmony.* New York: Oak Publications, 1968.
Randolph	Randolph, Vance. *Ozark Folksongs.* 1946-1950. Reprint. Columbia: University of Missouri Press, 1980.
Randolph and Cohen	Randolph, Vance, and Norm Cohen. *Ozark Folksongs.* 1 volume abridgement. Urbana: University of Illinois Press, 1982.
Richardson	Richardson, Ethel Park. *American Mountain Songs.* 1927. Reprint. New York: Greenberg, 1955.

Ritchie

Ritchie, Jean. *Singing Family of the Cumberlands.* 1955. Reprint. New York: Oak Publications, 1963.

Roberts (1974)

Roberts, Leonard, *Sang Branch Settlers: Folksongs and Tales of a Kentucky Mountain Family.* Austin: University of Texas Press, 1974.

Roberts (1978)

Roberts, Leonard. *In the Pine: Selected Kentucky Folksongs.* Pikeville, Kentucky: Pikeville College Press, 1978.

Rosenbaum

Rosenbaum, Art. *Folk Visions and Voices: Traditional Music and Song in North Georgia.* Athens: University of Georgia Press, 1983.

Scarborough

Scarborough, Dorothy. *On the Trail of Negro Folk-Songs.* 1925. Reprint. Hatboro, Pennsylvania: Folklore Associates, 1963.

Sharp

Sharp, Cecil J., and Maud Karpeles. *English Folk-Songs from the Southern Appalachians..* 2 volumes. London: Oxford University Press, 1932.

Shellans

Shellans, Herbert. *Folk Songs of the Blue Ridge Mountains.* New York: Oak Publications, 1968.

Talley

Talley, Thomas W. *Negro Folk Rhymes.* 1922. Reprint. Port Washington, New York: Kennikat Press, Inc., 1968.

Thede

Thede, Marion. *The Fiddle Book.* New York: Oak Publications, 1970.

Thomas

Thomas, Jean. *Devil's Ditties.* 1931. Reprint. Detroit: Gale Research Company, 1976.

Thomas and Leeder

Thomas, Jean, and Joseph A. Leeder. *The Singin' Gatherin'.* New York: Silver Burdett Co., 1939.

Warner

Warner, Anne. *Traditional American Folk Songs from the Anne and Frank Warner Col-*

lection. Syracuse: Syracuse University Press, 1984.

White   White, Newman Ivey. *American Negro Folk-Songs.* 1928. Reprint. Hatboro, Pennsylvania: Folklore Associates, 1965.

Biblio-discography

1. Songs About Love and Lovers

Little Birdie

A. Basic References

Brown III, 54-56.
Brown V, 28-29.
Roberts (1974), 157-58.
Roberts (1978), 221-23.

C. 78 RPM Recordings

The Coon Creek Girls	A.R.C. 04413
Vernon Dalhart	Columbia 15044

D. LP and Cassette Recordings

The Bray Brothers with Red Cravens	*Prairie Bluegrass.* Rounder 0053.
Willie Chapman	*Mountain Music of Kentucky.* Folkways 2317.
The Coon Creek Girls	County 712.
———	*Early Radio Favorites.* Old Homestead OHCS-14.
Vernon Dalhart	*Ballads and Railroad Songs.* Old Homestead OHCS-12.
The Greenbriar Boys	*Ragged But Right!* Vanguard VSD-79159.
Roscoe Holcomb	*The Music of Roscoe Holcomb and Wade Ward.* Folkways FA 2363.
Comer and Deborraha Mullins	*Over the Garden Wall.* No label name or number.

Ron Penix, Cathy   *Hammered Dulcimer Reunion.*
Barton and Jay Round   Take 2 T2P 001.
Glen Smith   *Clawhammer Banjo, Volume 3.*
   County 757.
Stanley Brothers   *Folk Concert.* King 834.
Hally Wood   *Songs To Live By.*
   Tannehill Records HW 101.

Prisoner's Song / Tragic Romance

A. Basic References

Brown III, 411-16.
Brown V, 246.
Burton and Manning I, 60-61.
Burton and Manning II, 62-63.
Cazden, Haufrecht, Studer, 371-76.
Combs and Wilgus, 227 (reference only).
Fuson, 143.
Henry (1938), 327.
Jones (1984), 154 (reference only).
Randolph III, 226-28.
Randolph and Cohen, 489-91.
Richardson, 55.

B. Other References

John Harrington Cox, *Traditional Ballads and Folk-Songs Mainly from West Virginia* (1939; reprint. Philadelphia: American Folklore Society, 1964), 193-94.
Charles J. Finger, *Frontier Ballads* (Garden City, New York: Doubleday, Page & Co., 1927), 129.
W. Roy MacKenzie, *Ballads and Sea Songs from Nova Scotia* (1928; reprint. Hatboro, Pennsylvania: Folklore Associates, Inc., 1963), 303.
Charles Neely and John W. Spargo, *Tales and Songs of Southern Illinois* (Menasha, Wisconsin: George Banta Publishing Co., 1938), 239.
Dorothy Scarborough, *A Song Catcher in the Southern Mountains: American Folk Songs of British Ancestry* (New York: Columbia University Press, 1937), 346.
Earl J. Stout, *Folklore from Iowa* (New York: The American Folklore Society, 1936), 87-88.

C. 78 RPM Recordings

Dock Boggs	Brunswick 133
Brierhopper Brothers	Champion 16602
Carter Family	Victor 23731
	Bluebird B-5096
Jesse Crawford	Victor 19980
Vernon Dalhart	Columbia 257-D
	Okeh 40328
	Brunswick 2900
	Supertone 2000
	Gennett 3030
	Silvertone 3030
	Herwin 75505
	Challenge 163
	Challenge 319
	Champion 15073
	Gennett 5588
	Silvertone 5588
	Edison 59459
	Victor 19427
	Victor 19426
	Cameo 703
	Romeo 241
	Pathe 032085
	Perfect 12164
	Emerson 10850
	Banner 0826
	Brunswick 6799
	Paramount 20440
	Emerson 3013
	Bell 340
	Columbia 563-D
Harmonians	Harmony 105-H
Wingy Manone	Bluebird B-7014
David Miller	Romeo 5954
	Conqueror 7709
	Paramount 3159
Riley Puckett	Columbia 15719-D
George Reneau	Vocalion 14991
	Vocalion 5056
Stanley Brothers	Blue Ridge 45-514

Weaver Brothers   Columbia 15487-D

D. LP and Cassette Recordings

Clarence Ashley and Tex Isley	Folkways FA 2350.
Dock Boggs	*The Legendary Dock Boggs Vol. I.* Folkways FA 2351.
Hylo Brown	*Hylo Brown Sings His Bluegrass Hits.* Jessup / Michigan. Bluegrass MB 134.
_____	*Early Bluegrass*. Anthology of Country Music ACM-6.
The Carter Family	*Vol. 3*. CMH 116.
Bill Clifton	*Wanderin'*. Hillbilly HRS 001.
Vernon Dalhart	*The First Singing Cowboy on Records.* Mark 56 793.
_____	*1925-1930*. Golden Olden Classics 702.
_____	*Old Time Songs*. Davis Unlimited DU 33030.
Colin Davies	*Cockney Music Hall Songs & Recitations.* Tradition TLP 1017.
Greenbriar Boys	*Better Late Than Never!* Vanguard VRS 9233.
Ernest Helton	*Folk-Songs of America:The Robert Winslow Gordon Collection, 1922-1932*. Library of Congress L68.
Kentucky Colonels	*Appalachian Swing*. World Pacific 1821.
_____	*Bluegrass Special*. World Pacific WPS 21898.
Del McCoury	*Del McCoury Sings Bluegrass.* Arhoolie F 5006.
Estella Palmer	*Stone County Singing*. Shoestring SGB 1.
Hank Snow	*Songs of Tragedy*. RCA Victor LPM 2901.
Stanley Brothers	*Together For the Last Time*. Joy 10329.
Earl Taylor	*Alan Lomax Presents Folk Songs from the Bluegrass*. United Artists UAL 3049.
_____	*The Bluegrass Touch*. Vetco LP 3017.

Pig in a Pen / Going to Little Creek

A. Basic References

Brown III, 145.
Brown V, 79-80.
Jones (1984), 229-30.

Lunsford and Stringfield, 44-45.
Randolph III, 184, 377.
Roberts (1974), 166-67.
Scarborough, 125.

B. Other References

William A. Owens, *Swing and Turn: Texas Play-Party Games* (Dallas: Tardy Publishing Company, 1936), 70-71.
Carl Sandburg, *The American Songbag* (New York: Harcourt, Brace and Company, 1927), 308-9.

C. 78 RPM Recordings

Bascom Lamar Lunsford	Brunswick 227
	Vocalion 5246
Fiddlin' Arthur Smith	Bluebird 7043

D. LP and Cassette Recordings

W.L. Gregory and Clyde Davenport	*Monticello: Tough Mountain Music from Southern Kentucky.* Davis Unlimited DU 33014.
Grandpa Jones Family	*Grandpa Jones Family Album.* CMH-9015.
George Pegram and Red Parham	*Music from South Turkey Creek.* Rounder 0065.
Fiddlin' Arthur Smith & His Dixieliners	*Volume 2.* County 547.
Stanley Brothers	*Folk Concert.* King 834.
————	*On Radio Volume One.* County 780.

Banjo Pickin' Girl

C. 78 RPM Recordings

Emry Arthur	Vocalion 5230
Dick Burnett	Gennett unissued
The Coon Creek Girls	Okeh 04413

D. LP and Cassette Recordings

Emry Arthur	*I Am a Man of Constant Sorrow.* Old Homestead OHCS-190.

Dick Burnett and	*A Ramblin' Reckless Hobo.* Rounder 1004.
Leonard Rutherford	
The Coon Creek Girls	*Banjo Pickin' Girl.* Rounder 1029.
_____	*Country & Western Classics: The Women.*
	Time/Life TLCW-02.
Lily May Ledford	*Banjo Pickin' Girl.* Green Hays GR712.
Helen Osborne	*Charlie Monroe on the Noonday Jamboree*
	—1944. County 538.

Look Up, Look Down That Lonesome Road

A. Basic References

Brown III, 347-48.
Brown V, 210.
Scarborough, 73.
White, 300-01.

B. Other References

Josiah Combs, *Folk Songs from the Kentucky Highlands* (New York: G. Schirmer, Inc., 1939), 28-29.

John A. Lomax and Alan Lomax, *Our Singing Country* (New York: The Macmillan Company, 1941), 146-47, 404.

Jim Morse, *The Dell Book of Great American Folk Songs* (New York: Dell Publishing Company, Inc., 1963), 235.

Dorothy Scarborough, *A Song Catcher in Southern Mountains: American Folk Songs of British Ancestry* (New York: Columbia University Press, 1937), 326.

C. 78 RPM Recordings

Svend Asmussen	Odeon 5243
Gene Austin	Victor 21098
Will Bradley	Columbia 35849
Tommy Dorsey	Victor 26508
Benny Goodman Quintet	Capitol 394
Group at State Farm,	Library of Congress AAFS14 B2
Boykin, South Carolina	
Lonnie Johnson	Bluebird 34-0714
Ted Lewis	Columbia 2181-D
Jimmie Lunceford	Vocalion 4831
Nat Shilkret	Victor 21996

| Muggsy Spanier | Bluebird 10766 |
| Sister Rosetta Tharpe | Decca 2243 |

D. LP and Cassette Recordings

| Group | *Afro-American Spirituals, Work Songs, and Ballads.* Library of Congress L 3. |
| Buell Kazee | June Apple JA 009. |

Bird Song

A. Basic References

Abrahams and Foss, 90-91.
Belden, 31-33.
Brown III, 203-05.
Brown V, 117-18.
Burton and Manning I, 105-06.
Davis, 202-03.
Morris, 197-98.
Randolph II, 355-57.
Sharp II, 304.
Talley, 183.

B. Other References

Arthur Loesser, *Humor in American Song* (New York: Howell, Soskin Publishers, Inc., 1942), 40-41.

Little Sparrow

A. Basic References

Abrahams and Foss, 88-89.
Belden, 477-78.
Brewster, 328.
Brown III, 290-93.
Brown V, 173-75.
Cazden, 16-17.
Combs & Wilgus, 227 (reference).
Cox, 419-21, 530.
Davis, 80-81.
Gainer, 142-43.

Henry (1938), 257-61.
Jones (1988), 148 (reference).
Lomax and Lomax, 90-91.
Morris, 366-68.
Owens (1950), 136-37.
Randolph I, 315-17.
Randolph and Cohen, 121-22.
Ritchie, 203-04.
Roberts (1978), 232-33.
Sharp II, 128-36.
Thomas, 82-83.

B. Other References

Celestin Pierre Cambiaire, *East Tennessee and Western Virginia Mountain Ballads* (London: The Mitre Press, 1934), 61, 98.

Mellinger Edward Henry, "More Songs from the Southern Highlands." *Journal of American Folklore* (1931): 100-02.

Arthur Palmer Hudson, "Ballads and Songs from Mississippi." *Journal of American Folklore* (1926): 119.

_____, *Folksongs of Mississippi and Their Background* (1936; reprint. New York: Folklorica, 1981), 167.

Josephine McGill, *Folk-Songs of the Kentucky Mountains* (New York: Boosey, 1917), 23-25.

Ethel and Chauncey O. Moore, *Ballads and Folk Songs of the Southwest* (Norman, Oklahoma: University of Oklahoma Press, 1964), 208-09.

Alton C. Morris, "Mrs. Griffin of Newberry." *Southern Folklore Quarterly* (1944): 172-73.

Isabel Nanton Rawn and Charles Peabody, "More Songs and Ballads from the Southern Appalachians." *Journal of American Folklore* (1916): 200.

Dorothy Scarborough, *A Song Catcher in Southern Mountains: American Folk Songs of British Ancestry* (New York: Columbia University Press, 1937), 313.

Hubert G. Shearin and Josiah H. Combs, *A Syllabus of Kentucky Folk-Songs* (Lexington, Kentucky: Transylvania Printing, 1911), 26.

Loraine Wyman and Howard Brockway, *Lonesome Tunes: Folk Songs from the Kentucky Mountains* (New York: H.W. Gray Co., 1916), 55-57.

C. 78 RPM Recordings

Carter Sisters and Mother Maybelle	Columbia 20820

D. LP and Cassette Recordings

Carter Sisters and Mother Maybelle — *Country & Western Classics: The Carter Family.* Time/Life TLCW-06.

Mary and Robert Gillihan — No label name 010069.

Mrs. Martha Hall — *Mountain Music of Kentucky.* Folkways FA 2317.

Alisa Jones — *Hammered Strings.* Cumberland C-8904.

Grandpa Jones Family — *Merle and Grandpa's Farm and Home Hour.* CMH-9032.

Leatherwoods — *Second Try.* No label name or number.

Edna Ritchie — Folk-Legacy FSA-3.

Jean Ritchie — *The Best of ...* Prestige/International 13003.

_____ — *A Folk Concert in Town Hall.* Folkways FA 2428.

_____ — *Kentucky Mountain Songs.* Elektra EKL 25.

Robin Roberts — *Come All Ye Fair and Tender Ladies.* Tradition TLP 1033.

Pete Seeger — *The Essential Pete Seeger.* Vanguard 97/98.

My Home's Across the Smoky Mountains

A. Basic References

Brown III, 326-27.
Brown V, 197-98.
Raim and Dunson, 40-41.
Roberts (1974), 150.
Rosenbaum, 11.

C. 78 RPM Recordings

The Carolina Tar Heels	Victor 40100
The Carter Family	Decca 5532
The Delmore Brothers	Bluebird 8247
Arthur Smith Trio	Bluebird 7221

D. LP and Cassette Recordings

The Carolina Tar Heels	GHP LP-1001.
———————	*Old-Time Music at Clarence Ashley's, Volume 2.* Folkways FA 2359.
The Carter Family	Ace of Hearts AH 112
Lawrence Eller	*Goin' to Georgia: The Eller Brothers and Ross Brown.* Flyright LP546.
Frank Proffitt	Folk-Legacy FSA-1.
Larry Richardson and Red Barker	*Blue Ridge Bluegrass.* County 702.
Pete Seeger and Frank Hamilton	*Nonesuch.* Folkways FA2439.

Free Little Bird

A. Basic References

Belden, 489.
Brown III, 293-97.
Brown V, 175-79.
Fuson, 130.
Jones (1984), 238.
Jones (1988), 118.
Owens (1950), 188-90.
Shellans, 24.

B. Other References

Louise Rand Bascom, "Ballads and Songs of Western North Carolina." *Journal of American Folklore* (1909): 240-41.

C. 78 RPM Recordings

The Allen Brothers	Victor 40266
Cousin Emmy	Decca 24216
Dykes' Magic City Trio	Brunswick 129
John Hammond	Challenge 332
McClendon Brothers and Georgia Dell	Bluebird 7339
J.E. Mainer's Mountaineers	King 5514
Land Norris	Okeh 45006

Ridgel's Fountain Citians	Vocalion 5389
Roane County Ramblers	Columbia 15498-D
Rutherford and Foster	Gennett 6746

D. LP and Cassette Recordings

The Allen Brothers	*When You Leave, You'll Leave Me Sad.* Folk Variety FV 12501.
———————	*The Chattanooga Boys.* Old Timey LP-115.
Bob Blair	*Not Far From Here: Traditional Tales and Songs Recorded in the Arkansas Ozarks.* Arkansas Traditions (no number).
Evo Bluestein	*Evo's Autoharp.* Greenhays GR-715.
Dykes' Magic City Trio	*Early String Bands, Volume 1.* Old Homestead OHCS 19.
Bascom Lamar Lunsford	*Music from South Turkey Creek.* Rounder 0065.
Bashful Brother Oswald (Pseud. for Pete Kirby)	*Banjo & Dobro.* Tennessee NR4990.
Roane County Ramblers	*Ballads and Breakdowns of the Golden Era.* Columbia CS 9660.
———————	*Complete Recordings, 1928-29.* County 403.

I Wish I Was a Mole in the Ground

A. Basic References

Brown III, 215-16.
Brown V, 124-26.
Jones (1984), 240.
Lomax and Lomax, 152-53.
Lunsford and Stringfield, 10-11.
Raim and Dunson, 84.
Rosenbaum, 167.

C. 78 RPM Recordings

Green Bailey	Conqueror 7255
Bascom Lamar Lunsford	Okeh 40155
	Brunswick 219

D. LP and Cassette Recordings

Bascom Lamar Lunsford   *Anglo-American Songs and Ballads.* Library
of Congress L 21.
_____   *Smoky Mountain Ballads.* Folkways FA 2040.

Beware, Oh, Beware

A. Basic References

Cohen and Seeger, 86-87.
Randolph III, 96.
Randolph and Cohen, 311-13.

C. 78 RPM Recordings

Blind Alfred Reed   Victor 23550

D. LP and Cassette Recordings

New Lost City Ramblers   *Folk Festival at Newport, Volume 2.*
Vanguard VRS-9063.
_____   *Old Timey Songs For Children.* Folkways
FC 7064.
Tom Paley, Mike Seeger,   *Sing Songs of the New Lost City Ramblers.*
and John Cohen   Aravel AB 1005.
Blind Alfred Reed   *How Can a Poor Man Stand Such Times and
Live.* Rounder 1001.

Darling Corie

A. Basic References

Burton and Manning II, 36-37.
Combs and Wilgus, 223 (reference only).
Fuson, 134.
Henry (1934), 102.
Jones (1988), 97.
Leisy, 76-77.
Lomax and Lomax, 392-93.
Roberts (1974), 154-55.
Sharp II, 204.

C. 78 RPM Recordings

Burl Ives	Okeh 6318
Buell Kazee	Brunswick 154
The Monroe Brothers	Bluebird B-6512
B.F. Shelton	Victor 35838

D. LP and Cassette Recordings

Logan English	*Kentucky Folksongs and Ballads.* Folkways FA 2136.
Mike Fenton	*My Privilege.* Heritage 053.
Roscoe Holcomb	*Close to Home.* Folkways FA 2374.
Buell H. Kazee	Folkways FS 3810.
Pleaz Mobley	*Anglo-American Songs and Ballads.* Library of Congress L14.
Pete Seeger	*Darling Corey.* Folkways FA 2003.
The Bill Sky Family	*Sweet Sunny South.* Heritage HRC 627.

Little Turtle Dove

A. Basic References

Belden, 479, 481, 482, 486.
Botkin, 284.
Brown III, 274-75.
Brown V, 157.
Cohen & Seeger, 60-61.
Combs & Wilgus, 227 (reference only).
Jackson, 63-64.
Jones (1984), 243.
Lunsford and Stringfield, 14-15.
Roberts (1978), 223-25.
Sharp II, 113-16.

C. 78 RPM Recordings

The Carter Family	Victor 20937
	Bluebird 6176
	Montgomery Ward 7021
Roy Hall and His Blue Ridge Entertainers	Vocalion 04717
	Conqueror 9230
Bascom Lamar Lunsford	Brunswick 229

Bascom Lamar Lunsford   Vocalion 5252

D. LP and Cassette Recordings

The Carter Family	*The Bristol Sessions.* Country Music Foundation CMF-011-L.
_____	*Early Classics.* Anthology of Country Music ACM 15.
_____	*Great Sacred Songs.* Harmony HL 7396.
Roy Hall and His Blue Ridge Entertainers	*Recorded 1938-1941.* County 406.
Bascom Lamar Lunsford	*Mountain Banjo Songs and Tunes.* County 515.
The A.L. Phipps Family	*Echoes of the Carter Family.* Pine Mountain PMR-248.

The Cuckoo

A. Basic References

Belden, 473-74.
Brewster, 346-47.
Brown III, 273-74.
Burton and Manning I, 66-67.
Cazden, Haufrecht, Studer, 146-47.
Cohen & Seeger, 62-63.
Cox, 425.
Davis, 82-83.
Huntington, 347-48.
Jones (1988), 129.
Lunsford and Stringfield, 54.
Randolph, 237-39.
Randolph and Cohen, 117-18.
Ritchie, 279-80.
Sharp II, 177.
Thomas, 153.

B. Other References

Peter Kennedy, *Folksongs of Britain and Ireland* (New York: Schirmer Books, 1975), 371.
Bradley Kincaid, *My Favorite Mountain Ballads and Old-Time Songs* (Chicago: WLS, 1929), 20.

Peter and Iona Opie, *The Oxford Dictionary of Nursery Rhymes* (Oxford: Oxford University Press, 1951), 139.

James Reeves, *The Everlasting Circle: English Traditional Verse Edited with an Introduction and Notes from the Manuscripts of S. Baring-Gould, H.E.D. Hammond and George B. Gardiner* (London: William Heinemann Ltd., 1960), 79-80.

James Reeves, *The Idiom of the People: English Traditional Verse from the Manuscripts of Cecil J. Sharp* (London: William Heinemann Ltd., 1958), 97-99.

Songs of All Time, revised edition (Berea, Kentucky: Council of the Southern Mountains, Inc., 1957), 9.

Asher Treat, "Kentucky Folksong in Northern Wisconsin." *Journal of American Folklore* (1939): 10-11.

C. 78 RPM Recordings

Clarence Ashley	Columbia 15489-D
Kelly Harrell	Victor 40047
Bradley Kincaid	Gennett 6620

D. LP and Cassette Recordings

The Apple Family	*The Apple Family with Wayne Clark.* No label name or number.
Clarence Ashley	*Anthology of American Folk Music, Volume 2.* Folkways FM 2952.
Bonnie Carol	*Fingerdances for Dulcimer.* Kicking Mule KM 220.
Mike Fenton and the Bill Sky Family	*Welcome to Galax.* Heritage HRC-078.
Kelly Harrell	*The Complete Kelly Harrell Volume I.* Bear Family 15508.
A.L. Lloyd	*The Foggy Dew and Other Traditional English Love Songs.* Traditional TLP 1016.
New Lost City Ramblers	*Volume 4.* Folkways FA 2399.
_____	*Old-Timey Music.* Disc D-102.
Joan O'Bryant	*American Ballads and Folksongs.* Folkways FA 2338.
Jean Ritchie	*Field Trip.* Collector Limited Edition CLE 1201.
_____	*Kentucky Mountain Songs.* Elektra EKL 125.

Jean Ritchie	*Singing Family of the Cumberlands.* Riverside RLP 12-653.
_____	*Sings the Traditional Songs of Her Kentucky Mountain Family.* Elektra EKLP-2.
_____	*World Festival of Folk Songs and Folk Dance.* Westminster WF 12008.
Robin Roberts	*Traditional Folk Songs and Ballads.* Stinson SLP 77.
Pete Steele	Banjo Tunes and Songs. Folkways FS 3828.

Time Draws Near

A. Basic References

Abrahams and Foss, 52-53.
Belden, 480-82.
Brown III, 299-304.
Brown V, 181-83.

D. LP and Cassette Recordings

| Dolly Greer | *The Watson Family Tradition.* Topic 12TS336. |
| Doc Watson | *Home Again.* Vanguard VSD 79239. |

2. Religious Songs

I'm Workin' on a Building

B. Other References

Dianne Dugaw, "'Dreams of the Past': A Collection of Ozark Songs and Tunes." *Mid-America Folklore* (1983): 65-66.
Howard W. Odum and Guy B. Johnson, *The Negro and His Songs: A Study of Typical Negro Songs in the South* (1925; reprint. New York: The New American Library, Inc., 1969), 72.

C. 78 RPM Recordings

| Camp Meetin' Choir with Deacon Tom Foger & Sister Bernice Dobson | Diamond D4 |
| The Carter Family | Montgomery Ward 4541 |

| The Carter Family | Bluebird 5716 |
| J.E. Mainer's Mountaineers | King 543 |

D. LP and Cassette Recordings

The Carter Family	Old Time Classics 6001.
————	*From 1936 Radio Transcripts.* Old Homestead OH90045.
————	*A Sacred Collection.* Anthology of Country Music ACM 08.
Dr. C.J. Johnson and His Family	*The Old Time Song Service Recorded Live in Atlanta, Georgia.* Savoy 14402.
The Stanley Brothers	*Old Time Camp Meeting.* King K-750.
Albertina Walker	*You Believe in Me.* Benson CO2673.

Go Wash in That Beautiful Pool

A. Basic References

Brown III, 624.

B. Other References

Louis W. Chappell, *Folk-songs of Roanoke and the Albemarle* (Morgantown, West Virginia: The Ballad Press, 1939), 169.

C. 78 RPM Recordings

| Reverend Moses Mason | Paramount 12702 |
| Dock Walsh | Victor 40327 |

D. LP and Cassette Recordings

| The Carolina Tar Heels | Folk-Legacy FSA-24. |

Twilight is Stealing

B. Other References

Albert E. Brumley, *Albert E. Brumley's Olde Time Camp Meetin' Songs* (Camdenton, Missouri: Albert E. Brumley & Sons, 1971), 61.
The Chuck Wagon Gang, *Our Recorded Songs Number Two* (No place given: The Chuck Wagon Gang, 1967), 83.

C. 78 RPM Recordings

The Stoneman Family   Victor (unissued)

D. LP and Cassette Recordings

Almeda Riddle   *How Firm a Foundation and Other*
                          Traditional Hymns. Arkansas Traditions
                          003.

I Will Arise

A. Basic References

Jackson, 232-33.

B. Other References

George Pullen Jackson, *White and Negro Spirituals: Their Life Span and Kinship* (New York: J.J. Augustin, 1943), 204.

C. 78 RPM Recordings

Reverend E.D. Campbell   Victor 35824

D. LP and Cassette Recordings

The Williams Family   *All in the Family.* Arkansas Traditions 004.

There Is a Happy Land

B. Other References

Original Sacred Harp (Denson Revision) (Cullman, Alabama: Sacred Harp Publishing Company, Inc., 1971), 354.

D. LP and Cassette Recordings

Almeda Riddle   *How Firm a Foundation and Other*
                          Traditional Hymns. Arkansas Traditions
                          003.

Sons of Sorrow

A. Basic References

Jackson, 51.

B. Other References

William Caldwell, *Union Harmony* (Maryville, Tennessee: n.p., 1837), no. 101.

D. LP and Cassette Recordings

Almeda Riddle   *How Firm A Foundation and Other Traditional Hymns.* Arkansas Traditions 003.

3. Children's Songs

Rockabye, Baby

A. Basic References

Brown III, 148-49.
Davis, 182.

B. Other References

James Orchard Halliwell-Phillips, *The Nursery Rhymes of England, Collected Chiefly from Oral Tradition.* 5th edition (London: F. Warne, and New York: Scribner, Welford, and Armstrong, 1853), 102, 157.

G.F. Northall, *English Folk-Rhymes: A Collection of Traditional Verses relating to Places and Persons, Customs, Superstitions, etc.* (London: K. Paul, Trench, Trubner & Co., 1892), 425-26.

Edward Francis Rimbault, *Nursery Rhymes, With the Tunes to Which They Are Still Sung in the Nurseries of England, Obtained Principally from Oral Tradition* (London: Cramer, Beale & Co., 1849), 17.

C. 78 RPM Recordings

George P. Watson   Edison 4036 (cylinder)

D. LP and Cassette Recordings

Love-A-Byes   Brentwood C5107N.

I Bought Me a Cat

A. Basic References

Brown III, 172-74.
Brown V, 102-04.
Davis, 187.
Morris, 418-19.
Randolph III, 36-39.
Randolph and Cohen, 290-91.
Richardson, 77.
Roberts (1974), 197-98.
Roberts (1978), 297-99.
Scarborough, 196.
Sharp II, 310.
Thomas, 156-57.

B. Other References

Robert Chambers, *Popular Rhymes of Scotland*. New edition (London and
    Edinburgh: W. and R. Chambers, 1870), 190.
Arthur Loesser, *Humor in American Song* (New York: Howell, Soskin,
    1942), 42-43.
William Wells Newell, *Games and Songs of American Children* (1883;
    reprint. New York: Dover Publications, Inc., 1963), 115.
Loraine Wyman and Howard Brockway, *Lonesome Tunes: Folk Songs
    from the Kentucky Mountains* (New York: H.W. Gray Co., 1916),
    6-13.

C. 78 RPM Recordings

Old Harp Singers   Musicraft 222-B
of Nashville, Tennessee

D. LP and Cassette Recordings

Bradley Kincaid   *Album Number One*. Bluebonnet BL 107.
_____   *Old Time Songs*. Old Homestead
                         OHCS-314.

Mike and Peggy Seeger   *American Folk Songs for Children.* Rounder
8001/8002/8003.

4. Songs for Social Occasions

Jennie Jenkins

A. Basic References

Brown III, 102-03.
Brown V, 51-53.
Browne, 416-17.
Flanders and Brown, 164-67.
Jones (1984), 241-42.
Lomax and Lomax, 86-87.
Lunsford and Stringfield, 18-19.
Owens (1950), 206-07.
Randolph III, 208.

B. Other References

Eloise Hubbard Linscott, *Folk Songs of Old New England* (New York:
Macmillan Company), 199-200.

C. 78 RPM Recordings

Bascom Lamar Lunsford   Folkways FP 40

D. LP and Cassette Recordings

Mr. and Mrs. E.C. Ball   *Anglo-American Shanties, Lyric Songs,*
Dance Tunes and Spirituals. Library of
Congress L2.
George and Ethel McCoy   *Songs of Childhood.* Library of Congress
LBC 13.
New Lost City Ramblers   *Old Timey Songs for Children.* Folkways
FC 7064.

Cindy

A. Basic References

Brown III, 482-85.

Brown V, 267-69.
Fuson, 172.
Gainer, 178-79.
Jones (1984), 230-31.
Leisy, 58-60.
Lomax and Lomax, 134-35.
Lunsford and Stringfield, 42-43.
Randolph III, 376-77.
Roberts (1974), 166-67.
Rosenbaum, 12-13.
Thomas and Leeder, 23.

B. Other References

James Pheane Ross, *Sing Kentucky* (Lexington: University of Kentucky, 1965), 20.

C. 78 RPM Recordings

Milton Brown and His Musical Brownies	Montgomery Ward 4536
Samantha Bumgarner and Eva Davis	Columbia 167
Fiddlin' John Carson	Okeh 45214
Vernon Dalhart	Perfect 12386
Ford and Grace	Okeh 45157
Al Hopkins and His Buckle Busters	Brunswick 105
	Okeh 40294
Bradley Kincaid	Supertone 9568
	Champion 15851
	Gennett 7112
	Superior 2770
	Brunswick 464
Lulu Belle and Scotty	Melotone 6-03-59
	A.R.C. 05487
Bascom Lamar Lunsford	Brunswick 228
Frank Luther Singers	Decca A-311
Shorty McCoy and His Southern Playboys	Bluebird 0511
Uncle Dave Macon	Vocalion 15323
	Vocalion 5099

J.E. Mainer's Mountaineers	Bluebird 7289
Pope's Arkansas Mountaineers	Victor 21577
Pete Seeger	Asch 432-4A
Gid Tanner's Skillet Lickers	Columbia 15232-D
Yale Glee Club	Columbia 6463

D. LP and Cassette Recordings

Roy Acuff	*On Radio 1953*. Golden Country LP-2202.
The Blue Sky Boys	*A Treasury of Rare Song Gems from the Past.* Pine Mountain PMR 305.
Homer Chastain, Calvin Chastain, & Don Holder	*In the Field: Traditional Fiddle Music from Southeast Tennessee.* Pine Breeze 005.
The Coon Creek Girls	*Early Radio Favorites*. Old Homestead OHCS-142.
The Hillbillies	*The Hillbillies*. County 405.
John Jackson	*Blues and Country Dance Tunes from Virginia*. Arhoolie F1025.
Bradley Kincaid	*Album Number Four*. Bluebonnet BL112.
_____	*Old Time Songs and Hymns Volume Four.* Old Homestead OHCS-317.
Lulu Belle and Scotty	*Early Country Harmony 1930s.* ACM-1.
Clayton McMichen and Riley Puckett	*Georgia Fiddle Bands Volume Two.* County 544.
Bruce Molsky and Bob Carlin	*Take Me As I Am*. Marimac 9023.
New Lost City Ramblers	*Volume 2*. Folkways FA 2397.
_____	*Volume 4*. Folkways FA 2399.
The Ozark Express	No label name or number.
_____	*Yester-Years*. No label name or number.
George Pegram and Red Parham	*Music from South Turkey Creek*. Rounder 0065.
Pope's Arkansas Mountaineers	*Echoes of the Ozarks Volume 1*. County 518.
The Russell Family	County 734.
Pete Seeger	*American Banjo*. Asch 352.
_____	*Country Dance Music Washboard Band.* Folkways FA 2201.
_____	*Folksay I*. Stinson SLPX 5.

Pete Seeger	Stinson SLPX 9.
	Stinson SLPX 12.
The Toast String	*Wanted.* No label name or number.
Ticklers	

Old Joe Clark

A. Basic References

Bayard, 98-99.
Botkin, 269-85.
Brown III, 120-24.
Brown V, 61-67.
Burton and Manning II, 37-38.
Combs and Wilgus, 91, 231 (reference only).
Cox, 495.
Gainer, 171-72.
Jones (1988), 114-15.
Lomax and Lomax, 124-27.
Owens (1983), 114.
Randolph III, 324-30.
Randolph and Cohen, 399-401.
Roberts (1978), 289-91.
Scarborough, 8, 125, 169, 192, 227.
Sharp II, 259.
Thede, 28-29.
Thomas, 106-07.
White, 28, 337.

B. Other References

Kathryn Blair, "Swing Your Partner!" *Journal of American Folklore* (1927): 97-98.
Paul G. Brewster, "More Songs from Indiana." *Southern Folklore Quarterly* (1940): 192-93.
Marie Campbell, "Play-Party Tunes and Fritter-Minded Ballads." *Tennessee Folklore Society Bulletin* (1939): 23.
Lila W. Edmonds, "Songs from the Mountains of North Carolina." *Journal of American Folklore* (1893): 131.
Ira Ford, *Traditional Music of America* (1940; reprint. Hatboro, Pennsylvania: Folklore Associates, 1965), 121.

James Orchard Halliwell-Phillips, *The Nursery Rhymes of England, Collected Chiefly from Oral Tradition.* 5th edition (London: F. Warne, and New York: Scribner, Welford, and Armstrong, 1853), 135.

Miles Krassen, *Appalachian Fiddle* (New York: Oak Publications, 1973), 16.

Arthur Loesser, *Humor in American Song* (New York: Howell, Soskin, 1942), 52-53.

Gene Lowinger, *Bluegrass Fiddle* (New York: Oak Publications, 1974), 12.

Lucien L. and Flora Lassiter McDowell, *Folk-Dances of Tennessee* (Ann Arbor, Michigan: Edwards Brothers, 1938), 76.

L.W. Payne, Jr., "Finding List for Texas Play-Party Songs"in *Round the Levee*, edited by Stith Thompson. Publications of the Texas Folklore Society, No. 1 (Austin: Texas Folklore Society, 1916), 35-38.

E.C. Perrow, "Songs and Rhymes from the South."*Journal of American Folklore* (1912): 152.

_____, "Songs and Rhymes from the South."*Journal of American Folklore* (1915): 176.

Vance Randolph, "The Ozark Play-Party."*Journal of American Folklore* (1929): 221-23.

Dorothy Scarborough, *A Song Catcher in Southern Mountains* (New York: Columbia University Press, 1937), 65.

C. 78 RPM Recordings

H.M. Barnes and His Blue Ridge Entertainers	Brunswick 313
The Hill Billies	Okeh 40376
	Vocalion 15369
Bradley Kincaid	Brunswick 485
	Conqueror 8090
McMichen's Melody Men	JD3511
W. Lee O'Daniel and His Hillbilly Boys	Vocalion 02975
Fiddlin' Powers and Family	Victor 19434
	Edison 51662
Fiddlin' John Carson	Okeh 40038
Riley Puckett	Columbia 15033-D
	Harmony 5146
Ernest Stoneman's Virginia Sorebacks	Victor 20302
Gid Tanner and His Skillet Lickers	Columbia 15108-D

DaCosta Woltz's   Challenge 333
Southern Broadcasters

D. LP and Cassette Recordings

Bob Anderson   *Indiana Hoedown*. Puritan 5003.
The Apple Family   *The Apple Family with Wayne Clark*. No
                          label name or number.
Chet Atkins and   *Reflections*. RCA AHL1-3701.
Doc Watson
Seth Austen   *Appalachian Fiddle Tunes*. Kicking Mule
                          KM 174.
Mark Biggs   *Not Licked Yet*. Centennial CCR-1981.
Boys From Indiana   *One More Bluegrass Show*. King Bluegrass
                          KB 545.
Camp Creek Boys   *The Camp Creek Boys*. County 709.
The Carter Family   *In Texas Volume 7*. Old Homestead
                          OHCS139.
Homer Chastain, Calvin   *In the Field: Traditional Fiddle Music from
Chastain, & Don Holder   Southeast Tennessee*. Pine Breeze 005.
Percy and Ida Copeland   *Harmonica, Volume 3*. No label name or
                          number.
Tommy Hunter   *Orange Blossom Special*. Prestige
                          International INT-13026.
Mark Jones and   *Second Generation Nashville*. Flying High
Dale Maphis   FH 7501.
Bradley Kincaid   *Favorite Old Time Songs 2*. Old Homestead
                          OHCS155.
Joe Maphis, Grandpa   *Merle & Grandpa's Farm and Home Hour*.
Jones, Merle Travis, Rose   CMH-9032.
Lee Maphis, Ramona
and Alisa Jones
Ozark Folk Center   *Volume 2*. OFC-2.
Staff Band
Wayne Perry   *American Fiddle Tunes from the Archive of
                          Folk Song*. Library of Congress L62.
Tilman and Molly Pyeatt   *Dance Around Molly*. No label name or
                          number.
Pete Seeger   *Country Dance Music Washboard Band*.
                          Folkways FA 2201.
                          Darling Corey. Folkways FA 2003.
_____   *The Essential Pete Seeger*. Vanguard 97/98.

Pete Seeger	*Frontier Ballads-Vol. II.* Folkways FA 2176.
_____	*Studs Terkel's Weekly Almanac on Folk Music.*
	Blues on WFMI. Folkways FS 3864.
The Simmons Family	*Wandering Through the Rackensack.* No label name or number.
Pam and Jean Simmons, Kay Blair, Pam Sanders	*Potpourri.* Dancing Doll DLP 612.
Ryan Thompson	*Ryan's Banjo.* Captain Fiddle Music 008.
The Toast String Ticklers	*Wanted.* No label name or number.
Wade Ward	*Anglo-American Shanties, Lyric Songs, Dance Tunes and Spirituals.* Library of Congress L2.

Cluck Old Hen

A. Basic References

Bayard, 237-38.
Jones (1984), 248.
Talley, 50-51.
Thede, 122-23.
Warner, 292-93.

C. 78 RPM Recordings

DeFord Bailey	Vocalion 5190
Fiddlin' John Carson	Okeh 4890
Bill Chitwood and Bud Landress	Silvertone 3050
Coleman & Harper	A.R.C. 8095
Homer Davenport and the Young Brothers	Challenge 110
George Edgin's Corn Dodgers	Columbia 15754-D
Fruit Jar Guzzlers	Broadway 8108
Grayson & Whitter	Champion 15629
Jess Hillard	Champion 16333
Al Hopkins and His Buckle Busters	Brunswick 175
Earl Johnson's Dixie Entertainers	Okeh 45123

Ruben Jones and the Short Creek Trio	Supertone 9176
Clayton McMichen	Joe Davis 3510
	Decca 2647
Fiddlin' Powers and Family	Edison 52083
Gid Tanner's Skillet Lickers	Columbia 110
Tennessee Ramblers	Brunswick 225
Unknown artists	Unissued Okeh test 81767

D. LP and Cassette Recordings

John Ashby — *Down on Ashby's Farm*. County 745.

Tom Ashley and Tex Isley — *Clarence Ashley and Tex Isley*. Folkways FA 2350.

Fiddlin' John Carson — *Old Hen Cackled and the Rooster's Goin' to Crow*. Rounder 1003.

Russell Cook — *Red Haired Boy*. Sword & Shield LPS 9201.

Kyle Creed and Fred Cockerham — *Clawhammer Banjo*. County 701.

Howdy Forrester — *Big Howdy Fiddling Country Style*. United Artists (no number).

J.P. and Annadeene Fraley — *Wild Rose of the Mountain*. Rounder 0037.

Neal Hellman — *Appalachian Dulcimer Duets*. Kicking Mule KM222.

Clint Howard, Fred Price and Their Sons — *The Ballad of Finley Preston*. Rounder 0009.

Grandpa Jones — *Family Gathering*. CMH-9026.

Ramona Jones — *Stone County Fiddlin'*. Happy Valley NR10274.

Leslie Keith — *Black Mountain Blues*. Briar BF-4201.

Clark Kessinger — *Fiddler*. Folkways FA 2336.

J.E. Mainer — *The Legendary J.E. Mainer Volume 8*. Rural Rhythm RRJEM 249.

——— *The Fiddle Music of J.E. Mainer and the Mountaineers Volume 19*. Rural Rhythm RJEM 227.

Hoyt Ming and His Pep-Steppers — *New Hot Times*. Homestead 103.

Eric Muller	*Frailing the Five String Banjo*. Sunny Mountain EB 100.
Frank Proffitt	Folk-Legacy FSA 1.
The Skillet Lickers	*Volume 1*. County 506.
Scotty Stoneman with the Kentucky Colonels	Briar SBR 4206.
Ryan Thompson	*Ryan's Banjo*. Captain Fiddle Music 008.
Doc Watson, Clint Howard, Fred Price	*Old Timey Concert*. Vanguard VSD 107/08.

Pretty Little Pink

A. Basic References

Botkin, 296-97.
Brown III, 110-12.
Brown V, 55-56.
Combs and Wilgus, 228 (reference only).
Davis, 219-20.
Jones (1984), 155 (reference only).
Jones (1988), 120-21.
Lomax and Lomax, 140-42.
Randolph III, 296-97, 309, 311.
Talley, 127.

B. Other References

Lila W. Edmands, "Songs from the Mountains of North Carolina." *Journal of American Folklore* (1893): 134.

Mellinger E. Henry, "More Songs from the Southern Highlands." *Journal of American Folklore* (1931): 89-90.

R. Emmet Kennedy, *Black Cameos* (New York: Albert & Charles Boni, 1924), 197.

James Mooney, "Folk-Lore of the Carolina Mountains." *Journal of American Folklore* (1889): 104.

Williams Wells Newell, *Games and Songs of American Children* (1883; reprint. New York: Dover Publications, Inc., 1963), 245.

Mary Wheeler, *Steamboatin' Days: Folk Songs of the River Packet Era* (1944; reprint. Salem, New Hampshire: Ayer Company, Publishers, Inc., 1984), 87-89.

C. 78 RPM Recordings

Frank Blevins & His Tar Heel Rattlers	Columbia 15210-D
The Hillbillies	Vocalion 5017
Bradley Kincaid	Supertone 9666
Bradley Kincaid	Brunswick 464
Prairie Ramblers	Bluebird 5322
	Montgomery Ward M-4471
Gid Tanner and His Skillet Lickers	Columbia 15709-D
Tenneva Ramblers	Victor 21645
West Virginia Coon Hunters	Victor 20862
Henry Whitter	Okeh 40077

D. LP and Cassette Recordings

Frank Blevins & His Tar Heel Rattlers	*Ballads and Breakdowns of the Golden Era.* Columbia CS 9660.
Samantha Bumgarner	*Banjo Songs of the Southern Mountains.* Riverside RLP 12-610.
O.L. Coffey	*Play and Dance Songs and Tunes.* Library of Congress AFS L9.
Buna Hicks	*Beech Mountain, North Carolina Vol. II.* Folk-Legacy FSA-23.
The Hillbillies	*A Fiddlers' Convention in Mountain City, Tennessee.* County 525.
Clint Howard	*Old Time Music at Clarence Ashley's.* Folkways FA 2355.
Tex Isley	*North Carolina Boys.* Leader LEA 4040.
Tommy Jarrell and Oscar Jenkins	*Down to the Cider Mill.* County 713.
Grandpa Jones	*Family Gathering.* CMH-9026.
Buell Kazee	*Sings and Plays.* Folkways FS 3810.
Bradley Kincaid	*Favorite Old Time Songs Volume 2.* Old Homestead OHCS-155.
Leatherwoods	*'Fourth' Coming.* No label name or number.
Bascom Lamar Lunsford	*Minstrel of the Appalachians.* Riverside RLP 12-645.

J.E. Mainer	*The Legendary J.E. Mainer, Vol. 13*. Rural Rhythm RRJEM 234.
Charlie Moore	*Sings Good Bluegrass*. Vetco 3011.
Comer and Deborraha Mullins	*Over the Garden Wall*. No label name or number.
New Lost City Ramblers	*Vol. 3*. Folkways FA 2398.
Ozark Folk Center Staff Band	*Vol. 2*. OFC-2.
George Pegram and Walter Parham	*Pickin' and Blowin'*. Riverside RLP 12-650.
Ola Belle Reed	Rounder 0021.
Hobart Smith	*Banjo Songs, Ballads and Reels from the Southern Mountains*. Prestige 25004.
Tenneva Ramblers	Puritan 3001.
Howard Wallace	*Old-Time Five String Banjo*. Jewel LPS 186.
West Virginia Coon Hunters	*Wonderful World of Old Time Fiddlers*. Vetco 102.

Drink 'Er Down

B. Other References

Arthur Loesser, *Humor in American Song* (New York: Howell, Soskin Publishers, Inc., 1942), 304-05.

5. *Songs of Work*

Roll On, John / Poor Rail Road boys

A. Basic References

Brown III, 267.
Brown V, 151-52.
Cohen, 575.
Combs & Wilgus, 233 (reference only).
Shellans, 47.
White, 139.

B. Other References

Robert Winslow Gordon, "Old Songs that Men Have Sung." *Adventure* (1924): 191.

Archie Green, *Only a Miner: Studies in Recorded Coal-Mining Songs* (Urbana: University of Illinois Press, 1972), 334-36, 342-44.

C. 78 RPM Recordings

Buell Kazee   Brunswick 144

D. LP and Cassette Recordings

The Greenbriar Boys   *Ragged But Right*! Vanguard VSD-79159.
Buell Kazee   June Appal JA 009.

Reuben

A. Basic References

Botkin and Harlow, 464-65.
Brown III, 264-65, 337-38.
Brown V, 148-50.
Burton and Manning II, 32.
Cohen, N., 503-17.
Combs & Wilgus, 230 (reference only).
Henry (1934), 424.
Jones (1984), 236.
Leisy, 240-41.
Lomax and Lomax, 326-29.
Warner, 309-10.

B. Other References

Louise Rand Bascom, "Ballads and Songs of Western North Carolina."*Journal of American Folklore* (1909): 244-45.
Robert Duncan Bass, "Negro Songs from the Peedee Country."*Journal of American Folklore* (1931): 431.
Bruce R. Buckley, "'Uncle' Ira Cephas—A Negro Folk Singer in Ohio."*Midwest Folklore* (1953): 14-15.
MacEdward Leach and Horace P. Beck, "Songs from Rappahannock County, Virginia."*Journal of American Folklore* (1950): 282-83.
Howard W. Odum and Guy B. Johnson, *Negro Workaday Songs* (Chapel Hill: University of North Carolina Press, 1926), 66.
E.C. Perrow, "Songs and Rhymes from the South."*Journal of American Folklore* (1913): 170-71.

Eric Sackheim, *The Blues Line: A Collection of Blues Lyrics* (New York: Schirmer Books, 1975), 314-15.

C. 78 RPM Recordings

Emry Arthur	Paramount 3237
	Paramount 3295
	Broadway 8216
Carolina Ramblers	Melotone 13047
String Band	Oriole 8345
	Perfect 13012
	Romeo 5345
Fiddlin' John Carson	Okeh 40196
Wilma Lee and	Columbia 21049
Stoney Cooper	
Cousin Emmy	Decca 23583
William Francis	Vocalion 1090
and Richard Sowell	
Grayson and Whitter	Gennett 6320
	Champion 15447
	Challenge 397
	Victor 21189
	Bluebird B-5498
Woody Guthrie	Stinson 627
Charlie Lincoln	Columbia 14272-D
Wade Mainer and	Bluebird B-8990
the Sons of the	
Mountaineers	
Wade Mainer,	Bluebird B-7298
Zeke Morris, and	
Steve Ledford	
Sonny Osborne	Big 4 Hits 24
Riley Puckett	Columbia 15563-D

D. LP and Cassette Recordings

Red Allen and the Allen Brothers	*My Old Kentucky Home*. King Bluegrass KB-523.
Emry Arthur	*Paramount Old Time Tunes*. JEMF 103.
Blue Grass Mountain Boys	*The 37th Old TimeFiddler's Convention*. Folkways FM 2434.
Bluegrass Tarheels	*The Bluegrass Tarheels*. United U625-S.

Dock Boggs	*Dock Boggs, Vol. 3.* Asch AH 3903.
Benny and Vallie Cain	*More of Benny and Vallie Cain.* Rebel SLP 1537.
Camp Creek Boys	*June Apple.* Mountain 302.
Kenny Cantrell and the Green Valley Boys	*Home Sweet Home Revisited.* SPBGMA 7601.
Fiddlin' John Carson	*Songs of the Railroad.* Vetco LP 103.
_____	*The Old Hen Cackled and the Rooster's Going to Crow.* Rounder 1003.
Bill Clifton	*Going Back to Dixie.* Bear Family BF 15000-2.
Fred Cockerham	*Down to the Cider Mill.* County 713.
_____	*Clawhammer Banjo.* County 701.
Randall Collins	*Randall Collins Stands Tall in Georgia.* Atteiram API 1015.
Elizabeth Cotten	*Shake Sugaree.* Folkways FT 1003 / FTS 31003.
Jenes Cottrell	*Old Time Music from Clay County, West Virginia.* Kanawha 301.
Country Gentlemen	*Folk Songs and Bluegrass.* Folkways FA 2410.
_____	*Yesterday & Today, Vol. 3.* Rebel SLP 1535.
Dan Crary	*Bluegrass Guitar.* American Heritage AHLP 275.
Dub Crouch and the Blugrass Rounders	*Grass Cuttin' Time in Missouri.* Missouri Area Bluegrass Committee LP 101.
J.D. Crowe and the Kentucky Mountain Boys	Lemco 609.
_____	King Bluegrass KB 524.
Hubert Davis and his Season Travelers	*Down Home Bluegrass.* Stoneway STY-115.
The Dillards	*Back Porch Bluegrass.* Elektra EKL 232.
Raymond Fairchild and the Maggie Valley Boys	*King of the Smokey Mountain Banjo Players.* Rural Rhythm RR-146.
Lester Flatt, Earl Scruggs and the Foggy Mountain Boys	*Foggy Mountain Banjo.* Columbia CS 8364.
_____	*The World of Flatt and Scruggs.* Columbia KG 31964.
_____ with Doc Watson	*Strictly Instrumental.* Columbia CL 2643 / CS9443.

Frosty Mountain Boys
with Raymond Fairchild
Josh Graves, Bobby
Smith, and the Boys
from Shiloh
Grayson and Whitter

———————

Wade Hill and the
Bluegrass Professionals
Smiley Hobbs

Thomas Holland and
the Crossroads Boys
The Holy Modal
Rounders

———————

John Jackson
Tommy Jarrell

———————

and Kyle Creed
Vester Jones

Bill Keith and
Jim Rooney
Kentucky Colonels
Mrs. Esco Kilgore

David Lambeth and the
High Lonesome Ramblers
Log Cabin Boys
Jim McCall
Maggie Valley Boys
Wade Mainer, Zeke
Morris, and Steve
Ledford
J.E. Mainer's Crazy
Mountaineers
Jimmie Martin

Mamma Likes Bluegrass Music. Rural
    Rhythm RR-FM159.
Josh Graves. Vetco 3025.

Going Down Lee Highway. Davis Unlimited
    DU33033.
*Old Time Southern Dance Music: the
    String Bands.* Old Timey X-100.
Revonah 503.

*American Banjo Tunes and Songs in Scruggs
    Style.* Folkways FM 2314.
Old Time Fiddling at Union Grove.
    Prestige Folklore 14030.
Prestige Folklore 14031.

Alleged in Their Own Time. Rounder 3004.
Vol. 2. Arhoolie F 1035.
Tommy Jarrell's Banjo Album. County 748.
June Apple. Mountain 302.

*Traditional Music from Grayson and Carroll
    Counties.* Folkways FS 3811.
Livin' on the Mountain. Prestige Folklore
    14002.
Livin' in the Past. Briar BT 7202.
Railroad Songs and Ballads. Library of
    Congress L61.

A Tribute to the Stanley Brothers. King
    Bluegrass KB535.
Rural Rhythm RR-184.
Pickin' and Singin'. Vetco LP 3010.
Rural Rhythm RR-170.
Smoky Mountain Ballads. RCA Victor
    LPV507.

Ball Mountain ALP 201.

Country Music Time. Decca 74285.

Kenny Miller, Mrs.
Miller and Mike Seeger

James Monroe

New Lost City Ramblers

_____

_____

Osborne Brothers

Peg Leg Sam

George Pegram

Pete Pike

Piney Ridge Boys

Poplin Family

_____

Frank Proffitt

Ola Belle Reed

Tony Rice

Art Rosenbaum

Earl Scruggs

_____

_____

Garland Shuping

Pat Sky

Ralph Stanley

Stanley Brothers

_____

_____

_____

_____

Don Stover

Stringbean

Virginia Mountain Boys

Cliff Waldron and the
New Shades of Grass

---

*American Banjo Tunes and Songs
   in Scruggs Style.* Folkways FA2314.

Live at Bean Blossom. MCA2-8002.

Country Music and Bluegrass at Newport.
   Vanguard VRS9146 / VSD79146.

Gone to the Country. Folkways FA2491.

New Lost City Ramblers with Cousin Emmy.
   Folkways FT1015 / FTS3101.

Number 1. CMH 6202.

Medicine Show Man. Trix 3302.

Rounder 0001.

Rebel R-1474.

Flat Land Bluegrass. King Bluegrass 553.

The Poplin Family of Sumter, South Carolina.
   Folkways FA 2306.

Melodeon MLP7331.

Folk-Legacy FSA 1.

*First Annual Brandywine Mountain Music
   Convention.* Heritage 6.

Guitar. King Bluegrass KB529.

5 String Banjo. Kicking Mule KM-108.

Dueling Banjos. Columbia C 32268.

His Family and Friends. Columbia C 30584.

Nashville's Rock. Columbia CS 1007.

*Garland Shuping on Banjo with the
   Bluegrass Alliance.* Old Homestead 90038.

Patrick Sky. Vanguard VRS 9179 / VSD 7917.

A Man and His Music. Rebel SLP 1530.

Great, Great, Great. King 994.

The Legendary Stanley Brothers, Vol. 2.
   Rebel SLP 1495.

16 Greatest Hits. Starday SD 3003.

Railroad Songs. King 869.

King 615.

The World's Finest Five String Banjo.
   King 872.

Things in Life. Rounder 0014.

Starday SLP 179.

Vol. 2. Folkways FA 3833.

Rebel 1502.

Howard Wallace	*When You and I Were Young.* Jewel LPS219.
Wade Ward	*The Music of Roscoe Holcomb and Wade Ward.* Folkways FA 2363.
	Uncle Wade. Folkways FA 2380.
Doc Watson and	*Old Time Music at Clarence Ashley's.*
Gaither Carlton	Folkways FA 2355.
_____ and	*The Watson Family Tradition* . Topic
Arnold Watson	12TS336.
Doc Watson, Clint	*Old Timey Concert.* Vanguard VSD 107/8.
Howard, and Fred Price	
Hedy West	Vanguard 9124.
Winnie Winston	*Old Time Banjo Project.* Elektra EKL 276.
Art Wooten	*A Living Legend.* Homestead 104.

6. *Comic Songs*

Ol' Coon Dog

A. Basic References

Brewster, 334.
Brown III, 132-34, 206-08.
Brown V, 119-21.
Combs & Wilgus, 223-24.
Jones (1988), 117-18.
Randolph II, 361.
Roberts (1974), 178-79.
Thede, 130.

C. 78 RPM Recordings

Bradley Kincaid	Brunswick 485
George Roark	Columbia 15383-D
Fiddling Doc Roberts	Gennett 6588

D. LP and Cassette Recordings

Fiddling Doc Roberts	Davis Unlimited DU33014.

Liza Up in the 'Simmon Tree

A. Basic References

Botkin, 295-96.
Brown III, 206-09, 522.
Brown V, 119-21.
Sharp II, 355.
Thomas, 91-93.
White, 172-74.

C. 78 RPM Recordings

Bradley Kincaid	Gennett 6761
	Champion 15687
	Champion 45057
	Supertone 9362
Tenneva Ramblers	Victor 21141

D. LP and Cassette Recordings

Bradley Kincaid	*Album Number One.* Bluebonnet BL 107.
_____	*Mountain Ballads and Old-Time Songs.* Old Homestead OHCS 107.
Tenneva Ramblers	Puritan 3001.

The Tobacco Song

A. Basic References

Burton and Manning II, 71.
Randolph III, 274-75.
Randolph and Cohen, 378-80.
Warner, 226-28.

B. Other References

Reprints from Sing Out!: Volume Eleven (New York: Oak Publications, 1968), 44-45.

D. LP and Cassette Recordings

Lena Armstrong   *The Traditional Music of Beech Mountain,
                         North Carolina Vol. II: The Later Songs
                         and Hymns.* Folk-Legacy FSA-23.

The Kicking Mule

A. Basic References

Brewster, 335-38.
Brown III, 567-68.
Brown V, 328.
Browne, 442-44.
Combs & Wilgus, 223-24.
Henry (1938), 430-33.
Jones (1988), 127.
Scarborough, 186.
Shellans, 76-77.
Talley, 47-48.
White, 157, 227-29.

B. Other References

Ira W. Ford, *Traditional Music of America* (1940; reprint. Hatboro, Pennsylvania: Folklore Associates, 1965), 295-96, 440-41.
Howard W. Odum and Guy B. Johnson, *The Negro and His Songs* (1925; reprint. New York: The New American Library, Inc., 1969), 238.

C. 78 RPM Recordings

Fiddlin' John Carson	Okeh 40071
John B. Evans	Brunswick 237
Georgia Yellow Hammers	Victor 40069
Sid Hampton	Columbia 15555-D
Al Hopkins and His	Brunswick 179
Buckle Busters	Okeh 40376
Bradley Kincaid	Gennett 6944
	Chamption 15787
	Supertone 9471
	Superior 2656
Logan County Trio	Supertone 9175
	Challenger 302

Uncle Dave Macon	Vocalion 5011
	Vocalion 15450
Chubby Parker	Gennett 6120
	Conqueror 7892
Bill Shafer	Vocalion 5413
Ernest V. Stoneman	Okeh 45036
Gid Tanner and His Skillet Lickers	Columbia 15237-D
Gid Tanner and Riley Puckett	Columbia 110-D
Arthur Tanner	Paramount 33166

D. LP and Cassette Recordings

Seth Austen	*Appalachian Fiddle Tunes*. Kicking Mule KM 174.
Henry King and Family	*Anglo-American Songs and Ballads*. Library of Congress L20.
John Taylor	*Laid Back Pickin'*. No label name or number.
Lois "Granny" Thomas	*In An Arizona Town*. Arizona Friends of Folklore AFF 33-3.
Lula Belle and Scotty	*Comedy Songs of LulaBelle and Scotty: Tender Memories Recalled, Volume III*. Mar-Lu 8903.

The Arkansas Run

A. Basic References

Belden, 426-28.
Cox, 254.
Lomax and Lomax, 76-77.
MacIntosh, 25-26.
Randolph III, 12-14.
Randolph and Cohen, 277-78.
Sharp II, 7.

B. Other References

Richard M. Dorson, *Buying the Wind: Regional Folklore in the United States* (Chicago: The University of Chicago Press, 1964), 530.

Austen E. Fife and Alta S. Fife, "Folk Songs of Mormon Inspiration."*Western Folklore* (1947): 48.

Lester A. Hubbard, *Ballads and Songs from Utah* (Salt Lake City: The University of Utah Press, 1961), 424.

Lilburn A. Kingsbury and Charles van Ravenswaay, "Some Old Time Songs."*Bulletin of the Missouri Historical Society* (1950): 488.

John A. Lomax, *Cowboy Songs and Other Frontier Ballads* (1910; reprint. New York: The Macmillan Company, 1938), 338-42.

Ethel Moore and Chauncy O. Moore. *Ballads and Folk Songs of the Southwest* (Norman: University of Oklahoma Press, 1964), 300-02.

Louise Pound, *American Ballads and Songs* (1922; reprint. New York: Charles Scribner's Sons, 1972), 175-76.

Carl Sandburg, *The American Songbag* (New York: Harcourt, Brace, 1927), 128.

C. 78 RPM Recordings

Cousin Emmy	Decca 24213
Tex Hardin	Champion 16552
Al Hopkins and His Buckle Busters	Brunswick 318
Lonzo and Oscar	Victor 20-2378
Clayton McMichen and Riley Puckett	Columbia 15686-D
Len Nash and His Country Boys	Brunswick 354

*Other books of interest
from August House Publishers, Inc.*

Laughter in Appalachia

Appalachia's special brand of humor—dry, colorful, and
earthy—from Loyal Jones and Billy Edd Wheeler.
ISBN 0-87483-031-1, HB, $19.95
ISBN 0-87483-032-X, TPB, $8.95

Curing the Cross-Eyed Mule

More from Jones and Wheeler—450 Appalachian jokes,
along with essays by Roy Blount, Jr., and William Lightfoot.
ISBN 0-87483-083-4, TPB, $8.95

The Preacher Joke Book

A surprisingly reverent collection of religious humor,
poking fun less at the message than at the messengers.
ISBN 0-87483-087-7, TPB, $6.95

Cowboy Folk Humor

Jokes, tall tales, and anecdotes about cowboys,
their pranks, their foibles, and their times.
ISBN 0-87483-104-0, TPB, $9.95

A Field Guide to Southern Speech

A twenty-gauge lexicon for the duck blind, the deer stand,
the skeet shoot, the bass boat, and the backyard barbecue.
ISBN 0-87483-098-2, TPB, $6.95

Gridiron Grammar

A handbook to understanding coaches, players, officials,
Monday-morning quarterbacks, and football widows in the South.
ISBN 0-87483-158-X, TBP, $6.95

Dog Tales

Some tall, some true, all collected from the oral tradition, these stories
do justice to our beloved canine friends. Just right for reading aloud.
ISBN 0-87483-076-1, TPB, $6.95

*August House Publishers, Inc.
P.O. Box 3223, Little Rock, Arkansas 72203
1-800-284-8784*